What Others Are

"*Motivational Leaders* is both delightful reading and immensely practical. Mastering its contents can be a quantum leap in your growth. Must reading!"

— Joe Batten, CPAE Speakers Hall Of Fame
Author, *Tough-Minded Leadership, The Master Motivator*
and *The Leadership Principles Of Jesus*

"I love the wonderful stories, great wisdom, and powerful strategies in this book. *Motivational Leaders* looks at both the human side and the leadership side of motivation in a very compelling way."

— Marci Shimoff
Co-author, *Chicken Soup for the Woman's Soul*

"A diverse and provocative view of the important but elusive relationships between leadership and motivation from people who have made this their life's work."

— Alan Weiss, Ph.D.
Author, *Million Dollar Consulting*

"This book, *Motivational Leaders*, provides skills, perspectives and wonderful insights into motivation and leadership. What a great resource to have the collected wisdom of so many proven leadership authorities in one place. It's a must read!"

— Ed Oakley, CSP
Author, *Enlightened Leadership*

"The secret for any successful leader is to be able to fully connect with people. *Motivational Leaders* goes beyond pure leadership strategies and provides tools for leaders to successfully connect at every level."

— Mary LoVerde
Author, *Stop Screaming At The Microwave*

"Our organization lives and breathes its mission and guiding principles. All 500+ employees have memorized the mission and practice implementing it daily. It is our constitution. *Motivational Leaders* provides invaluable knowledge to anyone wishing to do the same for their organization. Read it and then DO IT!"

– Dean Curtis
Chief Executive Officer
Chairman of the Board, Curtis and Associates

"A must-read for anyone aspiring to be a motivational leader."

– Patricia Fripp CSP, CPAE Speakers Hall Of Fame
Author of *Make It So You Don't Have to Fake It*

"The ideas in this book can help you become more motivated and become a better motivator. That's the essence of motivational leadership."

– Mark Sanborn, CSP, CPAE Speakers Hall Of Fame
Speaker and Author

"The lessons in *Motivational Leaders* are invaluable ... but the authors' stories and the illustrations are what really make this book come alive. It is a wonderful combination of "head" and "heart" information."

– LeAnn Thieman
Co-author of *Chicken Soup for the Nurse's Soul*

"Most great leaders lead by example. Here is a book full of them. Buy it — Read it — Put to work. You'll be one of those examples"

– W Mitchell, CSP, CPAE Speakers Hall Of Fame
Author of *It's Not What Happens To You,
It's What You Do About It*

THE ULTIMATE RESOURCE FOR MOTIVATING YOURSELF AND OTHERS

Strategies and Wisdom From America's Top Professional Motivators

Brian Biro • Susan Carnahan • Doug Cartland • Tom Doane
Doug Hanson • Ab Jackson • Tim Gard • Kevin Lust • Michele Matt
Ruby Newell-Legner • Vilis Ozols • Mike Schlappi • Laura Stack
Michael Staver • Bernadette Trujillo-Vadurro

www.MotivationalLeaders.com

Motivational Leaders
Strategies and Wisdom from America's Top Professional Motivators

Copyright © MM

Printed in the USA
Cover design and layout by: Ad Graphics, Inc., Tulsa, OK

Published by:
The Ozols Business Group
2002 Montane Drive East, Suite 3000
Golden, CO 80401
(303) 526-2400

Compiled by: Vilis Ozols, MBA, CSP

Library Of Congress Catalog Card Number: 00-191000
ISBN: 0-9679329-0-4

Additional copies of *Motivational Leaders*
can be obtained from any of the authors.

Author contact information follows each chapter.
Quantity discounts are available.

Additional products, services, links
and information can be found at
www.MotivationalLeaders.com.

Do you have a company meeting?
Does your organization have an annual event?
Do you attend a convention that could benefit from
one of these dynamic and powerful presenters?
Please feel free to contact any one of the authors
about having them present at your upcoming event.

Throughout the book you will see specific professional speaking designations that you may not be familiar with.

What is NSA: The National Speakers Association is a member association of the International Federation for Professional Speakers, with more than 5000 members, and is dedicated to advancing the art and value of experts who speak professionally.

What is CSP? The Certified Speaking Professional designation, established by NSA, is the speaking profession's international measure of professional platform skill. CSP is conferred only on those who have earned it by meeting strict criteria and indicates proven experience in what is required to deliver client satisfaction. Only 393 speakers worldwide hold this professional designation.

What is CPAE Speaker Hall of Fame® — NSA established the CPAE *Speaker Hall of Fame®* to honor professional speakers who have reached the top echelon of platform excellence. Admission into the CPAE *Speaker Hall of Fame* is a lifetime award for speaking excellence and professionalism.

Dedication

This book is dedicated to the spouses,
children, significant others, family, and
staff of the authors.
You are <u>our</u> "motivational leaders."
Without you, none of us could pursue the
amazing calling of being a
professional speaker and author.

– The authors

Acknowledgments

I must, first and foremost, thank and acknowledge the other fourteen co-authors for their time, effort, creativity and dedication to this project, Motivational Leaders. Every one of you is a true "motivational leader," but you are also more. You are visionaries for believing in this book at the idea stage. You are risk-takers for moving this project forward. You are so much more than "talkers," you are "doers," and you have the ability to move the world.

Immeasurable gratitude goes to Eric Chester, CSP, a consummate author, publisher, professional speaker and mentor. Your experience, insight and willingness to share were instrumental in this project.

Special thanks to Barbara McNichol, our project editor. No one will know all of the editing issues you corrected. Any errors left are mine alone.

To Jim and Barb Weems, at Ad Graphics, thank you for your invaluable contribution to this project in coordination, cover design, and layout. You are true professionals.

Mark Sanborn, CSP, CPAE, you are one of the most accomplished and prolific professional speakers of our time, yet you found time to contribute the introduction and enhance this book. Thank you.

Thanks to Joe Batten, CSP, CPAE, Dean Curtis, Patricia Fripp, CSP, CPAE, Mary LoVerde, W Mitchell, CSP, CPAE, Ed Oakley, CSP, Mark Sanborn, CSP, CPAE, Marci Shimoff, LeAnn Theiman and Alan Weiss, Ph. D., who agreed to review pre-edited work and share their words of endorsement.

I must thank the National Speakers Association and the Colorado Speakers Association and the countless members who have contributed to the personal and professional growth of so many of us professional speakers. This is where motivational leaders grow.

A personal thank you for the help of these supporters and mentors: Scott Friedman, CSP, Rick Butts, Tim Gard, CSP, Erika Ozolina, Silvija and Varis Purkalitis, Maureen Brooks, Jim Phillips, and Jean Marie Martini.

And to my *raison d'etre*, the motivational leaders of my life, Andra, Aldi, Tali and Raimond, thank you for supporting and putting up with a husband and Pappa who is not like the rest.

Vilis Ozols, MBA, CSP
Publisher, compiler, and contributing author

Table of Contents

Introduction

M otivation has been maligned. Hackneyed attempts to motivate, or instruct others on how to do it, have resulted in a negative perception. It's like someone once said: "Research has shown that if you laid all the motivational speakers in the world end to end....everybody would be happy."

Sometimes motivation is associated with lack of substance. Motivation gets its worst rap when we confuse some of the people who espouse motivation with the subject itself. On Saturday Night Live, the late Chris Farley created a motivational speaker character who "lives in a van down by the river." It was a comic send-up of the worst part of motivation: the person who preaches it but neither practices nor benefits from it.

Don't let cultural perceptions lead you astray. Remember that common sense is an oxymoron: if it is commonly held, it probably doesn't make much sense.

Motivational leadership, however, is not an oxymoron. Leaders in any enterprise or endeavor are evaluated on both the changes they help create and how they create those changes. Motivation is the fuel that makes people and organizations burn with passion to make the world different.

A leader who is unable to motivate, I suspect, may not be a real leader at all.

This book contains the perspective of many accomplished speakers and authors who have devoted themselves to the study of motivation. They understand personal motivation and how to motivate others. You have in your hands the cumulative expertise of decades of experience and work in the field of human motivation.

Much of my work and research for more than twenty years has been devoted to the subject of motivation. I am fascinated by what motivation is, and how we develop it for ourselves and others. The great accomplishments of history have been the result of men and women who were motivated to do great things.

I don't necessarily agree with everything each of the contributing authors says (nor do each of them completely agree with each other, I imagine). That's okay. We can all benefit from authors who challenge our beliefs and stimulate our thinking. The objective isn't agreement, but improvement. After all, the purpose of a book, according to Christopher Morley, is to trap the reader into doing his or her own thinking.

You've heard the saying, "Nothing ever happens until somebody sells something." In reality, nothing ever happens until somebody is motivated to make it happen. The ideas in this book can help you become more motivated and become a better motivator. That's the essence of motivational leadership.

Mark Sanborn, CSP, CPAE
Speaker and Author
President, Sanborn & Associates, Inc. —
An idea studio for leadership development.

PART ONE

Motivating Yourself

C H A P T E R 1

The Gift is NOW! That's Why We Call It the PRESENT

By Brian Biro

Brian Biro is a motivational leader. He exudes enthusiasm. He makes enthusiasm contagious. He is possibly one of the most motivated and enthusiastic people I know and as you read this chapter you will get a feel for the foundations of motivation that fuel his fire. More importantly you can learn from these to fuel your fire. – VO

*   *   *   *   *

When your values are clear,
your decision-making is easy.
– Roy "Walt" Disney

The Gift is NOW! That's Why We Call It the PRESENT

By Brian Biro

A t some time in our lives, each of us will ask the most important of all questions. Though most people wait until late in life, the impact of asking it now can transform your life.

The question is simply: "Have I lived a great life?" Boom! Instantly you'll know your answer. It will either be a resounding, joyful, "YESSSS!!!!" or a despairing, "Why didn't I? How did I allow myself to *miss* so much?"

The one, most important thing you can do that irrepressibly leads to "YESSS!" — and helps you live a rich and fulfilling life — is to become *fully present* with all that you touch. This will make the biggest difference for you as a parent, friend, teammate, teacher, businessperson, student, or any other role you may play in life. Being fully present means one hundred percent of your mind, body, and spirit are truly *there* with the people who are with you. You're focused on them in that moment.

That may not seem like such a big deal at first, but sometimes the best way to clearly see the impact of a principle is to take an honest look at its opposite.

Swept Up in Career

I'm not proud of it, but I have been a classic example of not being present with those I love most deeply at important times in our lives. Several years ago, when I was the vice-president of a major training company, I was totally swept up in my own career. I was so focused on my work that I left my home for the office every morning at 4:40 A.M. I just *had* to be the first one there. I found myself on the road teaching seminars or visiting our various franchise locations on many weekends. It wasn't at all uncommon for me to stay at the office much later than 6 p.m. on weekday evenings, as well.

That year I was VP was the year my oldest daughter, Kelsey, had just turned five. It was also her first year in kindergarten, one of those milestones that arrive with such anticipation, then pass in an instant.

Though our whole family was excited about Kelsey's beginning steps in school, I was so driven in my work, not once did I see her wake up and get ready for her day. Not once was I there to make her breakfast or drive her to kindergarten. Not once did I show up after school unexpectedly for a "dad and me" surprise. I thought about being there a hundred times but always managed to put it off. I rationalized that I'd make it up to her sometime soon.

Yet every night, when I walked in the house, I was met with the same miracle. My beautiful daughter stopped whatever she was doing as soon as she heard the door open, sprinted to me as fast as she could run, and literally leaped into my arms. As she hugged me with all her might, she looked up at me with her shining brown eyes and said, "Daddy, I love you so much! And Daddy, I *missed* you so much today!" Then she would gush with excitement as she told me about all the things that had happened to her all day. (And, if you remember, when you're five years old, cool things happen!)

And I missed it. I didn't hear a word she said.

Not Showing Up

You see, when I walked into the house, the only part of me that showed up was my body. My mind, heart, and spirit were back at the office or worrying about what I had to do tomorrow. I was *never* present.

This went on for days that ran into weeks that rolled into months. Then one morning as I drove to work before 5 a.m., it was as if God had decided enough was enough. I felt an intense tightening in my stomach, and the next thing I knew, tears began to well up in my eyes. I began to sob. I pulled over to the side of the road filled with a vision of Kelsey and the truth.

The truth was that my precious daughter had stopped running to me. And even if I managed to "wake up" enough in the evening to ask her, "What happened in your day?" her answer had become completely predictable: "Nothing," or "I don't know." At one time, she couldn't wait to tell me everything. Now it took a crowbar to pry any information from her. *Nothing* and *I don't know* come from *not* being present.

Unmistakable Message

Through my tears that morning, I saw for the first time what we communicate to others when we are fully present. *Our*

19

presence sends the unmistakable message: "You are important!" And not being present sends an equally powerful message — one that my precious daughter was receiving loud and clear. It cried out to Kelsey that she must not mean as much to daddy as all the "stuff" he does all day and thinks about all the time.

That morning, humbled by the realization of my selfishness and determined to become the kind of father Kelsey deserved, I changed the foremost goal in my life. It's a simple goal, yet one I had never heard before. Now, my number one goal as a father, husband, coach, speaker, writer, and human being is to be *fully present* as much as I possibly can. I realized that morning for the first time that the only way I can ever touch other people's lives is by being fully present with them.

To our children, our spouse, our teammates, customers, and anyone we seek to positively affect, the energy we communicate through our presence IS our example. Nothing speaks more clearly and honestly.

Living My Word

Soon after that pivotal morning, I made some major changes in my life. I decided I would not wait until my children were grown and gone to understand how important our time is together. I would stop taking my wife and all she brings to our lives for granted. Today, I am most often the one who wakes up the children, cooks their breakfasts, makes their lunches, and drives them to school. I limit the number of speaking engagements I will accept each month so I can live my word about being fully present for my family. My life has never been so abundant and balanced.

Professionally, the impact of being fully present can be no less striking than it is with your family. Think back to your most satisfying successes: projects or challenges you tackled with energy and performance that astounded you; relationships you built into wonderful, lasting connections; creative solutions you found to problems that originally seemed insurmountable. Undoubtedly your level of presence was extraordinary. Being present has an immense impact on the quality of your leadership, and the enthusiasm and motivation you will instill in those around you. As a leader, nothing is more important than building trust. And nothing is more important to building trust than being fully present for those you lead and serve.

You Can't Fake It

Do you know the best part about being present? You can't fake it! How long does it take you to know when someone is not fully present? You can even tell over the phone. Being present is not a technique. It is a *choice* that enriches your life like no other. And it is a decision you can make today.

Inch by inch, anything's a cinch! For the next thirty days, pick out one person in your life with whom you commit to be more present. That doesn't mean you have to spend more time with the person you've chosen. It simply means that when you are together, you set aside the newspaper and shut off the television. Look at that special person with fresh eyes and an open heart. Ask more questions, then stop, breathe, and actually *listen!*

Once you've experienced the deepened connection you've built from this first concentrated effort at being present, you'll be hungry for more. It will become a habit —the natural and automatic essence of your character.

With your spouse, best friend, or partner, here's another action you can take that will develop the habit of being fully present. Once a month for six months, participate with full positive presence in an activity your loved one chooses — even if it's something you would normally avoid like the plague!

Rather Be Rolled in Molasses

Wouldn't you know that when I made this commitment to my wife, the activity she selected was clothes shopping! Normally, I would rather be rolled in molasses and dipped in corn flakes than spend a day shopping for clothes in a mall. But, as Forest Gump put so eloquently, "a promise is a promise," so off we went to the mall.

Usually when I am dragged to department stores, I look for a chair in some hidden corner and resignedly wait out my "sentence." But today my commitment was to be fully present, be engaged, energized, and alive. Considering the activity was shopping, this would require some real creativity!

Luckily, not long before our day of shopping together, I had watched the Richard Gere-Julia Roberts movie "Pretty Woman." So when we arrived at the mall, I decided to step into the Richard Gere character from the film and playfully act as if I were the mega-millionaire, regally appraising each outfit my wife modeled for me. I had a blast! I was even able to be present virtually the entire time. More importantly, my wife felt loved, appreciated, and connected.

Richer by the Moment

How often do your responses to family, friends, or associates begin with "just a minute," "in a second," or "what?" Do you find yourself asking those around you to repeat themselves because you missed their first attempt to communicate with you? When your children or teammates seek your attention, do you often view them as interruptions rather than feeling delight at the opportunity to share some precious moments?

If you find yourself falling into any of these patterns, it's an important sign that your focus is drifting away from the present into the past or future. It's time to listen completely before formulating your responses. Turn up your tremendous powers of observation and seek to understand others with great heart, compassion, and unselfishness. As you do, your impact on others deepens and your enjoyment of life becomes richer by the moment.

The greatest gift you can give others is something you can offer in any moment all year round. Mother Teresa said, "It's not just what we do that makes the difference, *it's the love we put into the doing.*" The love we put into the doing IS our full presence. Give this gift wholeheartedly, determinedly, and joyfully every single day. You will be amazed at the transformation in your relationships, at the energy and spontaneity that flows naturally into your life, and at the expansion of love and joy that elevates your spirit in every precious moment. Remember,

> The past is history
>
> The future a mystery
>
> The gift is *now*
>
> That's why we call it the *present*!

Give Yourself the Gift of Presence

As vital as being fully present with others is to developing wonderful relationships, *being fully present with yourself is just as crucial to finding the ongoing peace of mind and spiritual energy required to live well.* A simple analogy I discovered as a swim coach helps us understand the gifts we receive from quiet moments of full presence with *ourselves.* The analogy reveals a principle essential to balance and excellence called *recovery.*

To be a champion freestyle swimmer, you must develop optimum mechanics in the underwater portion of the arm stroke, which is known as the "resistance" phase. Under water, you use a sculling motion to accelerate the maximum amount of water pressure you pull through under your body. This action propels you through the water and becomes the focal point for coaches and swimmers as they seek to improve performance. Most stroke technique suggestions from coaches aim at increasing efficiency in the resistance phase and pulling more water.

The resistance phase is like the "doing" parts of our lives — the initiative, personal power, and action we take to power through each day. However, there is a more subtle yet equally important phase in every complete arm stroke — the portion of each stroke that occurs *above* the surface, just after you release the water behind you. It's called the "recovery phase."

During this portion of the arm stroke, you lift your elbow behind you then reach out in front to catch the water for the next arm pull. It is in the recovery phase that swimmers must relax, refuel, and replenish.

No matter how powerfully we swim during the resistance phase, without an efficient recovery on each stroke, we will rapidly wear down and eventually our performance will diminish. But with an effortless recovery, we more than endure; we flourish.

The recovery is the "being" part of our lives — the perfect metaphor for quiet moments of peace when we give ourselves the opportunity to replenish. At first, recovery may not seem as spicy and flavorful as resistance. But in the long run, it is more nourishing. By developing our recovery phase well, we find a reserve of strength that empowers our spirit. It serves us emotionally as confidence and spiritually as faith.

Tune into Recovery Phase

The next time you watch a great athlete or performer, tune in to the "recoveries." I always marveled at how Michael Jordan used his "off switch" just as smoothly and efficiently as he used his "on." He wasted no energy when he had the opportunity to rest and recover. He never worked against himself. It was one of the secrets of his exceptional durability. Using his finely tuned recovery skills, he was always ready to explode to the basket or make the big defensive play when he was most needed.

You can develop the same skill so you are ready to give your best when you are most needed. Begin today! Take the time to replenish. Don't wait. Make it a daily habit as automatic and important as eating. Go for a walk in the woods, sit in the sunshine, or let the rain fall gently on your face. Take ten slow, deep breaths and truly relax. Spend time each day in prayer, visualization, or meditation. Get quiet. Write in your journal.

As you develop the habit of giving yourself quiet recovery time each day, you will discover that, in the moments you are fully present with yourself, you're in the loving presence of the ultimate coach who guides us all, God.

In these moments, you will feed your soul.

*   *   *   *   *

Brian Biro
Asheville, North Carolina

 Brian Biro is, above all, a team-builder. He is one of the nation's foremost catalysts for transforming a "getting by" mentality to an infectious eager spirit ... a critical ingredient both at home and in your career. Brian is the author of the internationally acclaimed *Beyond Success: The 15 Secrets of a Winning Life!* and *The Joyful Spirit: How to Become the Happiest Person You Know!* His newest book is *Through the Eyes of a Coach: The New Vision for Parenting, Leading, Loving and Living!*

Brian was rated #1 from over 40 National Certified Speakers at 4 consecutive INC. Magazine International Conferences. He has appeared on Good Morning America, CNN's Business Unusual, and the Fox News Network. One of his repeat clients described Brian best when he said, "Brian Biro has the ENERGY of a ten-year-old, the ENTHUSIASM of a twenty-year-old, and the WISDOM of a seventy-year-old. He is available for half-day, full-day, and keynote presentations.

Contact Information:
Brian Biro
1120 Burnside Drive • Asheville, NC 28803
Phone: (828) 654-8852
FAX: (828) 654-8853
E-mail: bbiro@att.net
www.brianbiro.com

CHAPTER 2

The Gift!

BY DOUG HANSON, MBA

The first thing you notice about **Doug Hanson** is that he is the apex of success. Handsome, rich, successful, articulate. He seems too good to be true. He is a gifted person. The second thing you notice is that in the face of all of these exterior trappings of success he has much more than all of this ... he has inner success. He is at peace with himself, he is humble, he is gracious, and he acknowledges his spiritual foundations. Doug Hanson is a person to learn from.   – VO

*   *   *   *   *

Tell me whom and what you love,
and I will tell you who you are.
– Arsene Houssaye

The Gift!

By Doug Hanson, MBA

I begin this chapter with a question and ask that you write down your answers before you continue. The question is "What are your gifts?" Or, more specifically, "What are your most unique and special qualities?" Please do this exercise before you continue; we'll be sure to come back to it.

Now allow me to tell the story about an event that happened when I was seven years old. To get its full impact, first understand that I had a reputation for being somewhat "mischievous." In fact, my parents were certain that the cartoonist for Dennis the Menace secretly followed my every move for new material. I was one of those kids who never looked for trouble … "It just found me!"

A Miracle Every Sunday

It was Sunday and, like every Sunday, our family went to church, a small country church near Houston with about 40 or 50 members. At our church, a "miracle" happened every week. That's right, a miracle every single week. You see, at exactly the moment when the preacher stood up to approach the pulpit, I would have to go to the bathroom. It was an unexplainable phenomenon!

Actually, it was all part of my plan. My motivation was simple. I didn't like sitting through the sermon so I needed a way to get out of it. Since the bathrooms were in the back of the sanctuary, all I had to do was excuse myself, wait a few minutes until my parents lost track of me, then sneak out the door while everyone was facing forward listening to the sermon. It worked every Sunday — another miracle!

On this particular Sunday, I was walking around outside, kicking rocks, licking sour weeds, and doing things little boys do to kill time. Then something caught my eye. It was a pipe sticking out of our church building and I was certain it had never been there before. Being a typical seven-year-old boy, I examined the pipe carefully and curiously. About two inches in diameter, this pipe was sticking out about eight inches from the brick wall. "Why was this pipe here?" I wondered.

Continuing my inspection, I looked inside the pipe, but it was pitch black. So I put my ear to the pipe and, to my surprise, I could hear someone talking but I couldn't make out what was being said. It was as if the person was too weak to speak clearly and therefore just mumbled. Remember, I'm seven years old and *cool stuff* happens when you're seven. So I concluded that someone was "trapped" in our church building and desperately needed *my help* to get out!

Establish Communication

Ask any search and rescue professional what is the most important element of a rescue and you'll learn that establishing communication tops the list. This made sense to me so I took action and yelled into the pipe "helloooooooooooo." (I later learned that the voice I heard was the preacher's and the pipe was the overflow drainpipe for the baptismal.)

Now imagine a little blonde-haired boy yelling into a pipe. Also imagine how my seven-year-old voice sounded as it traveled down this long drainpipe. It exited the other end with a much deeper than normal tone, like the bass singer in a quartet, "HELLOOOOOOOOO."

Everyone inside the building froze, including the preacher. And the same question was on everyone's mind, including the preacher's…. "Was that the voice of God?" Well, everyone was confused except one person. My mother! She buried her face in her hands for she knew immediately that her mischievous, seven-year-old son had become *The Voice of God*!

I put my ear back onto the opening of the pipe to listen. It was completely quiet now. "The trapped person heard me but is waiting for more communication," I thought. So I did it again, only a much louder, "**HELLOOOOOOOOOOOO!!**" I looked in the pipe again but it was still pitch black. Then it occurred to me, "Maybe the person trapped inside could see the bright sunlight," so I shouted, **"CAN YOU SEE THE LIGHT?"**

As you can imagine, I had initiated a full-fledged revival inside. This sight has never been equaled since in our small town. Meanwhile, I was so excited about my discovery that I could hardly stand it. I was certain I was going to be a hero when I felt my father's hand pick me up by the scruff of my neck. He explained in his own special way that I was making a huge mistake. I soon returned to my seat with a tender bottom and tear-stained cheeks while the preacher restored order and went on with the service.

"Doug, Come With Me"

Afterwards, as the congregation filed out of the church, the preacher and my parents stood side by side. He shook their hands and thanked them for coming while my parents apologized for the ruckus. I was embarrassed and more than ready to go home. Just when I thought it was finally over, the preacher motioned me with his index finger to "come here." As he did this, he said in a firm, commanding tone, "Doug, come with me." With a serious look on his face, he took my hand and led me to his office. I couldn't believe it… I'd hit an all time low. "Not a spanking from the preacher, too?"

As I entered his office, I didn't look up at all. I didn't want to see his face. All I could see were his knees and feet. When he began to kneel, I raised my head slowly. To my surprise, he had a twinkle in his eyes and a smile on his face. He put his hands on my arms just below my shoulders, looked me in the eyes, and said, "Doug, you are a special young man. God has such big plans for you. I don't know what they are, but I do know you have a gift and you are going to make a difference." Then he gave me a great big hug and just held me for a moment.

Needless to say, I was excited. This was much better than a spanking! I'm not sure if he really believed I had a gift or if he just sensed that I needed a positive thought, but his true motivations are unimportant. The end result was that he planted a seed. A seed of awareness!

On the Fast Track

Twenty years later, that seed began to take root. I was working for a large computer company as a top salesperson. I had earned some degrees and was on the corporate fast track where everything revolves around money, title, and influence. At this stage, I felt confident I had all the answers. That's when our company sent the entire sales force to an outdoor experiential learning facility, also known as a ropes course.

On this day, I was being my normal self — having fun, making people laugh and, more importantly, helping them find the courage to participate in some challenging activities. I was cheering and yelling like a wild man and completely engrossed in helping one particular person when, all of a sudden, I felt a light touch on my shoulder. I looked and saw someone's arm around me. As I followed the arm up, I discovered it was attached to a man named Terry Henderson.

Terry was our main speaker the prior day; he had totally inspired all of us. He holds a Ph.D. in psychology and also owned and operated the ropes course. Terry had a presence about him that was magical, almost pristine. In his late 50s with white hair, he had a permanent smile on his face. One could tell he was at peace with himself and the world, like he had some special experiences and secrets about life. I highly respected him although I didn't know him at all. When I looked up to see what he wanted, he smiled a very loving and genuine smile as if he put extra effort into it just for me. He was *fully present* and I felt important. When my curious eyes met his, he pointed at me and said something that ultimately changed my life, forever. He said, "You've got it!" Then he walked away!

He knew exactly what he was doing because what do you think I did? You're darn right. I followed him around like a little puppy. I wanted to know what I had, and more important than that, could it kill me! *By arousing my curiosity, Terry inspired me to go in search of my gift.*

"You've Got the Gift"

After my repeated inquiries he finally stopped walking, put his hand on my shoulder, smiled at me again, and offered a little more. This time, in a quiet, almost whispery voice, he said, "You've got it… You've got the gift!" Then he began walking again. Being a young man in my twenties, short on priorities, wisdom and finances, I just had one question: "How much does the gift pay these days?" With that question in mind, I followed him some more, and I'm still following him today.

Terry took me under his wing and taught me much about life, success, priorities, giving back, family, faith, God, love, friendship, happiness, humility, and many other qualities. Terry especially taught me much about leadership. And my payback has far outweighed the financial rewards I originally sought.

Shortly after I began working with Terry, I remembered my preacher's words. He also said, "You've got the gift." Then I thought about other people throughout my life who positively influenced me, including Brian Biro, another author in this book. All of them, at one time or another, told me, "You've got the gift." It began to sink in. I have a gift! At first this was exciting. Then it became frustrating. What is my gift? That question is life changing!

Inspired Me to Search

I came to learn that I had many gifts, *and so do you*. Each of these leaders in my life may have been referring to something different, but it doesn't matter what they saw specifically. Ultimately, they inspired me to search.

These two stories illustrate what leaders do that set them apart from others. Leaders get both *massive results* and *massive rewards* from the same action — it is a foundational aspect of leadership. *They help people identify, develop, and use their gifts*.

Before these important people and others like them changed my focus, my whole life's significance came down to tangible results: how much money I made, what degrees I had, what titles I earned, etc. I remember this as the most stressful time of my life because my identity was always at risk based on my next action. My whole outlook — and ultimately my whole life — changed after I began recognizing my potential and searching for ways to use my gifts to make a difference in the world.

Here's what I know: *When people seriously understand their purpose and begin the journey to develop their gifts, they remove the daily stress associated with performance-based goals. They focus their energies instead on who they are becoming.*

Start with a Vision

Now that you've looked at the questions for yourself, ask the people you care about most, "What are your gifts? What are your most unique and special qualities?" You'll be amazed at how many people you absolutely love and adore reply with comments like "There is nothing special about me. I'm as ordinary as they come." This is a tragedy that needs your full attention because everything starts with vision. You simply can't "outperform" your self-image.

If you're honest with yourself, you may find you answered the questions the same way. Or, to avoid answering them, you skipped the exercise all together. If I accomplish nothing else with this chapter, I hope I can help you see that God didn't make any mistakes. He never said, "Oops... didn't mean to make that guy." I'm here to tell you, *that didn't happen.*

So, then, what gifts did God give you? Humor, intellect, athletic ability, music, romance, art, writing? You must keep searching for the answer yourself and, what's just as important, you must help others keep searching. Both actions will change your life!

Opening Minds

Terry Henderson, Brian Biro, and my preacher are leaders. Why? Because they made me feel special and they opened my mind to new possibilities. It's amazing what opportunities open up when you approach every day, every event, and every person from the mindset of "I'm searching for my gift."

I'm always amazed, however, when I hear people say they are waiting for God to "provide" the answers. Certainly we should seek God's wisdom and direction but here's a revelation for you: God does not work *FOR* us, He works *THROUGH* us. He is the ultimate leader and He knows the joy of life is found in the "search" for what you can become. He wants us to help each other discover our gifts and He allows uncertainty to exist because it is the most exciting component of the game. Like an awesome mystery waiting for your involvement to unravel the clues, it is truly the game of your life!

Unfortunately, many don't want to play unless they know the outcome. This is because they approach life from a performance-based mindset. They are afraid to fail. This is when leaders step in and make the difference. Leaders help others recognize that results are a temporary aspect of the game; they change every day. But personal vision lasts!

All leaders have their special qualities. Qualities like ethics, integrity, enthusiasm, popularity, motivation, intelligence, etc. vary from leader to leader. One important attribute that all proven leaders have, however, is the ability to inspire people to do more than they ever dreamed they could. They do this by creating a personal vision and encouraging them to get passionate about their future.

Leaders know that *we all have the gifts;* the world opens up to those who never stop searching and developing those gifts.

Plant Seeds for Others

Now it's your turn to plant some seeds. Take a few minutes to be *fully present* and recognize the qualities you respect most in your spouse, friends, neighbors, or co-workers. Then tell them. You can approach them with, "You've got it...You've got the gift." Let them be curious for a moment, then share your thoughts. At first they will feel uncomfortable and will downplay your assessment. But you'll also see a little pride beaming through as their imagination begins to run with the vision you are planting in their mind. Of course, most seeds won't take root with just one comment. You will have to be persistent. You'll have to recognize every success, no matter how big or small.

Eventually, these people will begin to *own* their new identity. When that happens, watch out... because they are going to soar!

*   *   *   *   *

Doug Hanson, MBA
Katy, Texas

Doug Hanson is a nationally recognized speaker, consultant, and performance coach who has helped corporations, sports teams, and individuals from all walks of life reach new heights of fulfillment and success. Everyone who meets Doug immediately recognizes his energy and passion for life.

Before starting his speaking career, Doug worked as a show director for ESPN sporting events, Director of Operations and Marketing for SuperCross motorcycle racing events, and spent 9 years in the computer industry as an enterprise sales and marketing professional for Toshiba, Texas Instruments and Hewlett Packard, where he was recognized as part of the annual elite sales team seven times.

Doug started his speaking and consulting company in 1994 to **help people** find happiness and to **help companies and sports teams** develop a winning culture. Whether he's serving as a motivational speaker, personal coach, or business consultant, Doug makes learning and improving fun. As a speaker, Doug has worked alongside a who's who list of famous speakers and for some of America's top companies. For 7 years Doug was a featured facilitator at Tony Robbins' Life Mastery University in Hawaii, and in 2004, Doug was the only motivational speaker chosen by the NFL Superbowl Host Committee to train 6,000 volunteers and 200 captains at the pregame rally in Reliant Stadium, two weeks prior to Superbowl XXXVIII.

Doug holds a B.S. degree in computer science from Sam Houston State University and a MBA from the University of Houston where he graduated with honors. Doug is from Katy, Texas where he lives with his bride of 20 years and their four children.

Contact Information:
Doug Hanson, MBA
3106 Huntington Court • Katy, TX 77493
Phone: (281) 391-7532
FAX: (281) 391-7539
E-mail: doug@doughanson.com
www.doughanson.com

C H A P T E R 3

It's All About Results

By Michael Staver, M.A.

Michael Staver is a mover and a shaker. He is one of those people who can talk about doing it and also make it happen by doing it. When you need results at a conference or a meeting, Michael is a catalyst to get results. How does he do this? Very simply, he has a bottomless capacity to help people. Enjoy this opportunity to share in his words. – VO

* * * * *

Genius is the ability to put into effect what is in your mind.
– F. Scott Fitzgerald

It's All About Results

By Michael Staver, M.A.

We live in a culture of change. It is a simple fact. All the clichés do little to help the anxiety and frustration people feel about the lack of stability that change brings.

I have heard it said that we should "embrace change." Asking someone to embrace change is like asking a turkey to embrace Thanksgiving. It's not likely to happen. The key to dealing with change is to understand one simple principle: it's all about results.

Ask yourself these questions: Are you achieving the results you want in your life? Are you seizing the goals, the ambitions, the dreams that a fulfilled and exuberant life is all about? Or have you allowed yourself to find "excuses" not to have that ideal job or fulfilling relationship? Is your life so busy, you forget about your hopes and dreams?

An article in *USA Today* reported responses from the general public to this question: "How many times do you think about quitting your job in a week?" The most frequent answer was an astounding three times a week. (Hopefully you're not thinking, "Wow, only three.")

If most Americans wish they could quit their jobs three times a week, that is a sad commentary on how things have changed. It used to be you came to work and knew what your job was. You got a performance review, maybe even a raise. On a good year, you also earned a promotion.

New Job Expectations

Now, you might come to work and get asked to jump into a new project. You say, "Sure. Can I have some people to help me out?" They answer, uhhhhhhh no! "Well, how about giving me some additional time then?" They answer, uhhhhhh no! "Well, how about some more money to make it worth the extra time and energy?" They answer, uhhhhhh definitely not. "What do you expect me to do?" Uhhhhhh we expect you to do it better, faster, cheaper, make the customer happy, and don't complain about it!

I believe that, given the appropriate opportunity and strategy, most people would work to achieve better results. The key is having the courage to look at those areas of your life and taking the necessary action to make results happen. If you're already living a good life, achieving good results, and moving ahead, then what needs to happen for you to move to the next level? All great champions continue to strive for higher levels of achievement. It is important to remember that the champion is the one who, in the face of winning, works diligently to improve and stay on top.

How to Get and Stay on Top

To achieve the results you want, keep your focus on these essential steps:

1. Determine your desired results.
2. Choose the appropriate strategy.
3. Take action.

Seems easy, doesn't it? Decide *what* you want, figure out *how* to get it, then *go get it!*

But if it were that easy, you would be living on some island sipping fruity drinks while your yacht was being cleaned. Though achieving success is not always easy, the steps to get there are that simple. Yet, many people get the steps mixed up and wonder why they fail to get the results they once found so attractive.

Settling for Less

It is reasonable to assume you will not always get the results you seek. So when that happens, which of the three steps do most people change — the results, the strategy, or the action?

Unfortunately, they tend to change their picture of the results they want rather than the strategy or action. It's called "settling for less" — changing the results because they have difficulty figuring out the appropriate strategy or action. They try once or even twice, fail, and give up.

How many of your dreams are left unfulfilled because you say, "I would but I just don't know how?" If people really knew *how* to overcome the things that block them from achieving outstanding results, they would do them. Most people just don't know. I saw a button recently that said, "Keeping your nose to the grindstone and your shoulder to the wheel simply gives you a flat nose and a sore shoulder." I love that! It is not about doing what you're doing better; it is about figuring out how to do it differently.

But let me be perfectly clear on this point: FORGET ABOUT THE HOW!! It is more important to focus on THE WHAT. What is the result you seek? Do you want to make more money? Be in a more fulfilling relationship? Attain better physical health?

When you get clear about each result, the appropriate strategies will start to show up. But you must state each result clearly and emphatically so it sounds like this: "I WILL lose 10 pounds in the next 60 days" rather than this: "In the next couple months, I am going to try to lose weight." Your brain responds best to detailed commitment, especially when it has a clear picture to follow.

See the Picture First

Here's an example of how it works. My step dad really enjoys jigsaw puzzles. Personally, I can't sit still for 10 minutes, much less the *hours* it takes, to put pieces of painted cardboard together. Regardless, one day I watched him go through the process of putting a puzzle together and was fascinated by what I saw.

Very methodically, he took the box, opened it, and dumped the pieces on the table, then proceeded to turn all of them over. Before he actually started, he took a quick look at the box top and formed a visual for how the puzzle would look when finished. Next, he dove in to the adventure. I noticed he went about placing pieces in a calculated way — edges first, then corners, and so on. So after getting a clear picture in his mind, all that remained was putting the pieces together.

I trust you are drawing some parallels here. It is crucial to SEE the picture and then begin to put the pieces together to achieve success. You also need to feel it, smell it, taste it, touch it. You must be drawn with great anticipation to it. And then you must take swift and immediate action. If you notice the strategy is failing, do not waiver in your pursuit of the result you want. Simply change the strategy.

New Year's Resolutions

An example of changing the result so the strategy makes sense is the never ending, always present, seldom achieved, New Year's resolution. You know, those commitments made at the end of every year. "This year it's going to be different. This year I'm finally going to lose weight. This year I'm finally going to get in shape. This year I'm finally going to stop smoking. This year I'm finally going to get married. This year I'm finally going to get a divorce. This year I'm finally going to have children (or this year I'm finally going to get rid of my children)."

Let's take getting in shape as an example of a New Year's resolution. I decide that, this year, I'm finally going to get in shape. So I join one of those gyms that takes money out of my checking account whether I show up or not. I go to the local sporting goods store and buy my new workout apparel to prove to everyone I've never been to a gym in my entire life. I buy my cross trainer workout shoes so I don't have to change shoes between workout activities. I set my alarm for 5:00 a.m. and go to bed with visions of firm muscles dancing in my head.

Then the alarm goes off. All of the sudden, a voice sounds off in the back of my head. It says...HIT THE SNOOZE BUTTON!

Now I don't know about you, but I set my alarm clock thirty minutes early to get three bonus snooze-button hits. The alarm goes off the first time and there is no problem because I know I have two snooze-button hits left. By the second time the alarm buzzes, I start to feel moody. Finally, by the third time the alarm goes off, the voice in my head comes back and engages in very destructive thought patterns.

It starts rationalizing! Rationalizing is simply making excuses for strategies that don't work. In my workout example, rationalizing would sound like this: "You know, Dr. Cooper at The Cooper Clinic says you only need 90 minutes of total aerobic workout in a week to keep your heart in good condition. This is Friday; why rush it?" Then that rationalization evolves into this one: "Why would a person rather stay in bed with the covers pulled up than go to the gym, sweat, and throw up?"

Pain and Pleasure as Motivators

You see, there are only two real motivators: the avoidance of PAIN and the pursuit of PLEASURE. I believe that staying in bed *is* less painful and more pleasurable than working out. And you know what? That's true in the short run. The challenge is to do the things that have the highest probability of achieving your desired results REGARDLESS of how it feels to do them.

Taking that concept further, the two key elements in achieving results are *frustration tolerance* (the ability to tolerate people, places and things that frustrate you) and *impulse control* (the ability to control your urges — like staying in bed instead of working out). If you master these two areas, the chances of getting the results you want increase. Is it challenging to learn them? Of course. But then so was walking when you were just learning to do that.

You get ahead by being firm in your results and flexible in your strategy, and by taking action regardless of how you feel. Do this by picturing the long-range outcomes — both positive and negative — of your current pattern. If you stay in bed with the covers pulled up and never go to the gym, what is the long-range cost of that behavior? Consider this picture without excuses or rationalizing. Feel, sense, taste, and touch the long-range consequences of staying in bed. This approach will compel you to act. And if it doesn't, it will at least free you from the burden of coming up with excuses when you have a heart attack or another avoidable physical trauma.

Attack, Don't Retreat

In the unabridged dictionary of military terminology, I have been told there are two words that do not appear: retreat and surrender. Do not retreat or surrender in the pursuit of your life's purpose. Instead, get intense about achieving your desired results.

Take charge! Attack the hill and you will find success through the following six steps. I remember them by using the acronym ATTACK to explain the steps required to achieve dramatic results.

A– Accept your circumstances as they actually are! If you are going to get "there" you must know and accept where "here" is. Remember, I did not say "resign yourself" to where you are; I said "accept" the circumstances you live in today.

T– Take responsibility! Understand that achieving results is up to you. Use the support and resources available to you, of course. But know this: excuse-free living will be your primary power tool for success. As long as we try to fix the blame, we can never fix the problem. Excuse-free living returns the control to you. It frees you from the victim mindset and propels you toward the results you want.

T– Take action! All the thinking and planning in the world will not help unless you do something. Discover what you want and advance toward it. Anything that moves you to the target is a step toward results. Don't hesitate and wait until everything is perfect.... JUMP. Once your ship starts moving, then you can adjust the course.

A– Acknowledge progress! People tend to spend too much energy focused on what they haven't accomplished. Instead, give yourself credit. Every little move you make toward desired results needs to be acknowledged. Start by giving yourself credit for caring enough to read this book.

C– Commit to new habits! A lifelong commitment to personal growth and development keeps you fresh and on top of your game. Develop a plan. Do at least one thing a month to learn something meaningful to you. That doesn't mean just doing "stuff." Practice what it takes to develop a habit, and use that habit to your best advantage.

K– Kindle new relationships! The word kindle has been defined as "to give new life to." When you follow these steps, you will give new life to all your personal and professional relationships.

Life continually provides opportunities. I challenge you to seize those opportunities and run with them. Most of them are in you now right now. Do not allow yourself to be consumed by excuses. Identify the results you want, determine a strategy, and start taking action today!

* * * * *

Michael Staver
Fernandina Beach, Florida

 Energy, Passion, and Focus are the words most commonly used when people describe their experience with Mike Staver. He maintains a speaking and consulting calendar of over 120 engagements per year. Michael's audiences consistently rate his programs and delivery over a 9 on a 10 point scale.

Michael has an uncanny ability to make the most complex ideas simple and memorable. His sense of humor, depth of knowledge and caring attitude make him one of the most inspiring speakers you will ever meet.

With a master's degree in counseling psychology and a bachelor's degree in business administration, he understands the importance of results and can coach your organization in the successful pursuit of its objectives. Here is an opportunity to work with a person who has coached many individuals and organizations in helping them establish strategies to reach their goals.

Contact Information:
Michael Staver
The Staver Group
Fernandina Beach, FL
(904) 321-0877
E-mail: mstaver@TheStaverGroup.com
Web Site: www.TheStaverGroup.com

CHAPTER 4

The 330 Burnout

BY AB JACKSON

Ab Jackson has a nature that is immediately obvious to everyone he comes into contact with, from the thousands in his audiences to his circle of friends. He has an immense capacity to share. This, coupled with his remarkable ability to explain, teach and connect is what makes him such a successful presenter. He is a motivator and a mentor for all who come in contact with him.   – *VO*

*   *   *   *   *

The quality of a person's life is in direct proportion to their commitment to excellence, regardless of their chosen field of endeavor.
– Vince Lombardi

The 330 Burnout

BY AB JACKSON

I could never beat the two cousins. At least twice a year, I would race them at track meets. We ran the 440-yard dash — one full lap around the track. Even though I did well in most other meets, I could never beat the two cousins. It was the way I ran that prevented me from triumphing over them.

I would get off to a very fast start. I wanted to be running first when I got to my dad. My dad always took time off work to come see me run. He liked to stand near the gate at the 110-yard marker to cheer me. As I ran by my dad, he would always yell, "Come on boy!"

And boy, did I come on. That cheer would propel me into a big lead at the 220 mark (half way through the race). Many times, my big lead would discourage the other runners and they would fall back. Even though I tired at the 330 mark (three quarters into the race), my lead would usually hold at the end. But not with the two cousins.

They'd stay close and when we got to the 330 mark, they would yell "330 burnout" to let me know they were coming. Then they'd both pass and finish ahead of me. I never finished higher than third place in a meet with the two cousins. Until one day when my life changed forever.

"We Have Your Number"

I remember looking for my dad as the race was starting, but he wasn't in his usual spot. I also remember looking over at the two cousins. They grinned back as if to say, "We have your number, buster."

The gun sounded and I got off to a great start. (I always got off to a great start.) I sprinted into the lead at the 220. (I was always in the lead at the 220.) The two cousins raced right behind me as we neared the 330 and I began to tire. They yelled "330 burnout!" and began to pass.

At that moment, my dad, now standing on the sidelines at the 330 marker, yelled, "Come on boy!" And boy did I come on (because I always turned it on when my dad cheered). That cheer propelled me past the two cousins and I won the race by ten yards — my fastest time ever and one of the fastest in our school's history.

My dad came over and shook my hand. My coach ran over, beaming, and said, "Congratulations! That was a great race. Do you know what just happened here?"

"Not exactly," I said, "but if you can bottle it, I'll take a case."

He laughed and said, "It's my fault. I just haven't seen it before. You always start strong. Today you finished strong. There was no '330 burnout.' We need to develop a new game plan for you. From now on, you are going to run smarter." He took out a 3X5 note card and wrote as he talked.

Four Keys to Success

"It's the basics that we forget," he said. "Remember the three Rs — reading, (w)riting and (a)rithmetic? They were simple to remember. Your plan has four keys to success. First, get off to a good start. Next, evaluate and adjust to keep moving forward. Third, have a strategy to cope with burn-out, stress and discouragement. And finally, finish strong."

I kept that card for years. Those four keys helped me run smarter through high school and college. And they have also served me in my business and personal life. Here's how they can help you.

The First Key —
Get Off To A Good Start

Already you are thinking, "Well, that lets me off. I have been in my present job for five years. It's too late for a good start for me."

I wouldn't be too sure about that. One of the worst things that happens in a job is getting too comfortable. In the old days, you just got fired; today you get right-sized, out-sourced, down-sized, or (my favorite) re-engineered (choo-choo!). *USA Today* calls it the "de-layering of the organization."

One survey says Americans change jobs every 2.5 years. Another predicts five-to-seven career changes in a working lifetime. So let's assume getting off to a good start becomes important to you in the near future, if not now. How do you do you do it?

1. Study

The American Library Association estimates the average American reads .5 books a year, or one half book per person per year! The most commonly heard reasons for not reading are "too little time" and "watching TV."

I have good news and bad news. First, the good news: you can do something about the TV set. Then the bad news: there is not much you can do about time. Given the limited time you have, here's how to improve your reading efficiency:

- Take a speed-reading course. I recommend ones that include retention of what you read as well as focusing on speed. Learning to speed read was the smartest money I have ever spent on skill-building.

- Read a variety of books. Add inspirational and self-help books to your list of books to read. I also recommend reading a biography every month. A wise person once said if we can't learn from the mistakes of past, we are doomed to repeat them.

- Read a different magazine each week. Buy a journal and record two good ideas from each of those magazines. At year's end, you will have 100 new ideas for success that you didn't have when the year began. Include a mix of magazines to vary your ideas: one week, read a sports magazine; next week, read a gardening magazine.

- Read to people who can't read — sight-impaired, illiterate, or children.

- Listen to audio books. One survey puts the average American in a car for more than 300 hours a year. That's the equivalent of a semester of college. I suggest listening to Jim Rohn, Zig Ziglar, Jeanne Robertson, Tom Peters, Ken Blanchard, Kevin Leman, and Cherie Carter-Scott. Listen to each several times—repetition increases retention. Keep your journal nearby to record the good ideas.

2. Plan

Next, do some planning. Start with the big picture first by doing the "Ten-Year Count Back." Get away to a quiet area with a legal pad and pen, then visualize yourself ten years in the future. Write down what you weigh, what you do for a living, where you live, what car you drive, and so on.

Be specific. (For example, what color is that car?) Take about 30 minutes altogether. Review your ten-year picture, then repeat the exercise for five years into the future. Repeat the exercise once more for one year from now. Dr. Stephen Covey calls this "beginning with the end in mind."

Once you have a clear picture where you are going, write short-range goals to get you there. Write them as if they have already happened. Say you weigh 160 pounds and want to lose 25 pounds in a year. Then you'd write, "On 12/31/01, I weigh 135 pounds." Say you want to read a book a month. You'd write, "On 12/31/00, I have finished book number 12." Recording these is critical; an insurance-industry study estimates only 3% of all Americans take time to put their goals in writing.

Having long-term and short-term goals helps keep you focused. Zig Ziglar uses an analogy of an archery contest with the greatest archer of all time. You could outshoot that archer if you blindfolded him and spun him around several times and then let him shoot. "That's silly," people would say, "how can you hit a target you can't see?" Similarly, how can you achieve your goals if they are not clear?

Study and plan your long-range and short-range goals. As Admiral James Stockdale said, "Education is an ornament in times of prosperity and a refuge in times of adversity."

The Second Key —
Evaluate Your Progress and Adjust

With your goals clearly in mind, daily planning and tracking is important. When I coached a minor league baseball team (the young ones, just out of T-Ball), one player came up and asked me, "Who's winning?" I said, "We are." He asked, "What's the score?" I said, "6 to 4." He asked, "Who's got 6?"

Clearly, this is a player not involved in the game. How can you be prepared to adjust if you don't keep score? When firefighters enter a room filled with heavy smoke, they don't say, "Well, we didn't feel like fighting fires today." No, they grab a mask, evaluate the situation, and adjust. Lives depend on their ability to do so!

These tips will help you stay in the game:

- Make daily plans and write them down. Your to-do list should include personal as well as professional tasks. I recommend first listing your tasks without ranking them, then prioritize by using A, B or C. ("A" tasks are most important, "B" tasks are next in line, "C" tasks are least important.) Next, estimate the amount of time the tasks should take. Build a cushion into your estimate; if you think it takes an hour to type the budget, estimate an hour and ten minutes. Finally, check those tasks off with Gusto!

- Use a planner, either a journal-type or an electronic one that best suits your lifestyle. Keep your to-do list in your planner. Customize it by adding sections for month-at-a-glance, telephone numbers and addresses, commitments you make and others have made to you, and projects you are tracking.

- Plan when you are at your best. Many people wait until the end of the day to plan for tomorrow. A morning person should plan in the morning; an evening person who works best after 2:00 p.m. should plan at the end of the day.

- Evaluate and adjust using the "LUST CHECK." Author Kevin Lust suggests stopping all activity and asking these four questions at regular intervals:

    1. What have I done so far?

    2. Is it right? (Have I been doing my "A" tasks?)

    3. Where do I stand now? (At three o'clock, I have ten items left on my to-do list.)

    4. What do I do next? (What's the best use of my time? What are the highest priorities?)

- Put the LUST CHECK on a 3X5 card, carry it with you, and do a LUST CHECK at least four times a day. J. C. Penny once said, "My eyesight is failing, but my vision is perfect." With the LUST CHECK, you'll find your vision is perfect while your evaluating-and-adjusting practice keeps you in the race.

The Third Key —
Cope with Burnout and Fatigue

Football coach Vince Lombardi once said, "Fatigue makes cowards of us all." A key to success is having a strategy to deal with stress, burnout, fatigue, and discouragement — all of which are inevitable. It's known that 66% of primary health care visits are stress related. Americans spend 115 million dollars a week on stress-related medication and American business will spend 300 billion dollars on stress-related causes in the year 2000.

To prevent burning yourself out, do these activities:

- Rest and exercise. In *The Corporate Athlete*, author Jack Groppel observes the lack of exercise in adulthood (results in) increases in depression, moodiness, anxiety, fatigue, insomnia, and muscle weakness. Exercise makes you feel better, look better, and cope better. Experts recommend 45 minutes of aerobic and anaerobic exercise daily.

- Laugh more. In *Stress For Success*, Jim Loehr says, "Every laugh is a wave of recovery. In a real sense, laughter is a form of internal jogging." So read a funny book each week. If you read it before bed, you'll sleep better. Watch a funny movie. Keep a humor file of cartoons and stories funny nearby. Call your funny friends — chances are they have a new joke to lighten your day.

- Get enough rest. Experts suggest eight hours of rest a day. During the day, take short breaks. Remember first grade? After lunch and play, we grabbed our blankets and rested. We were refreshed for the rest of the day. (I sure miss my blanket!)

59

- Have a daily quiet time. Devote thirty minutes each day to inspirational readings, bible study, prayer, or meditation. Dr. Ken Blanchard calls this "connectedness."

- Have a cheerleader. My dad moved from the 110-yard mark to the 330 mark where I really needed encouragement. Find someone to do the same for you, then tap into that power when you need it.

The Fourth Key —
Finishing Strong

Will Rogers once said the average life of a politician lasts "until he is found out." Finishing strong requires character. Character is who you are when no one is looking.

These tips help you develop character and finish strong:

- Right relationships. In Homer's *Odyssey*, Odysseus leaves for war, entrusting care of his young son to Mentor who served as teacher and overseer of young Telemachus. Seek a mentor who has maturity and skill in areas with which you struggle. As you develop your skills, become a mentor yourself. Look for a Telemachus who is eager to learn. Stephen Covey calls mentoring part of leaving a legacy.

- Right Reasons. A mission statement answers four questions: Who am I? What do I do? For whom do I do it? Why do I do it? A mentor of mine suggests asking this question when making daily decisions: "Is that which I am about to do moving me closer to or farther away from my mission?"

- Right Risks. Pastor Roger Barrier says, "Be a participant, not a spectator." Growth requires risk. Some of the strongest words in the Bible are for the man who wasted his talent (Matthew 25:33). Here are some risks worth taking:

1. Join Toastmasters. It teaches conquering fear and communicating effectively. Toastmasters is the most supportive and encouraging club you will ever belong to.

2. Volunteer for a tough assignment at work. One expert even suggests accepting a demotion or lateral move if it means acquiring new, valuable, marketable skills.

3. Call customers you lost last year. Ask them to come back. And ask how you can do a better job next time.

4. Start a business. Remember the statistics regarding job and career changes? What's your passion? Will it serve others? Go for it!

- Right Reputation. Author and mentor Kevin Leman, in *Winning The Rat Race Without Becoming A Rat*, advises employers to "hire character, not characters." Right reputation means:

I. Making and keeping commitments.

II. Respecting the ideas and opinions of others.

III. Setting high standards for yourself and having high expectations of others.

IV. Making difficult choices and accepting the consequences.

Success in life is not running the "330 Burnout." All endeavors require a good start, evaluation and adjustment, stamina to handle the burnout, and finishing strong.

"On your mark......................"

* * * * *

Ab Jackson
Tucson, Arizona

 Ab Jackson has been a catalyst for change in organizations worldwide. His over 1500 presentations in board rooms, on stage, and in training departments have provided life changing how-to's for nearly 250,000 people. To understand "how-to's" consider the two titles of his best selling audiocassette programs—*How to Organize Your Life and Get Rid of Clutter* (CareerTrack) and *How to Manage Multiple Projects, Meet Deadlines, and Achieve Objectives* (Nightingale/Conant).

He speaks on such varied topics as Making Better Decisions, Excelling as a Supervisor, Team Building, Reading Faster and Remembering More, and Humor in the Workplace. The groups he has presented to, include; Inland Revenue of New Zealand, Thorn EMI of Great Britain, Cable and Wireless of British Virgin Islands, Farmers Insurance, MCI, VISA, Chevron, the cities of Glendale, California; Schaumberg, Illinois; Reno, Nevada; and Des Moines, Iowa, US Air Force, US Navy, VA Hospitals, Bureau of Indian Affairs, Tufts Veterinary School, and the State of Ohio Transportation Department.

Prior to his speaking career, Mr. Jackson worked in banking and insurance for 18 years. He also was a play-by-play sports broadcaster. He won the State of Arizona Humorous Speech Contest. Ab is an associate with Great Game Associates, part of the Great Game of Business. He is also president of Abstract Consulting. Mr. Jackson's favorite audience is his wife of over 26 years, Dede, and his two sons, Wesley and Scott. The Jackson's live in Tucson, Arizona.

Contact Information:
Ab Jackson
P.O. Box 68210 • Tucson, AZ 85737
Phone: (520) 797-0942
Message/FAX: (520) 544-4767
E-Mail: abjbasebal@aol.com

CHAPTER 5

Bulletproof Principles for Striking Gold

BY MIKE SCHLAPPI, MBA

A wheelchair is not what makes **Mike Schlappi** who he is. When you first meet him, the most noteworthy feeling is that you wish you could have this person be your friend. He is extraordinary in so many ways. Friendly, talented, accomplished, an amazing athlete, and yet, he has an endearing balance of humility and pride. He also has a story to tell; the wheelchair is just the vehicle. — VO

* * * * *

In the depth of winter,
I finally learned that within me
there lay an invincible summer.
– Albert Camus

Bulletproof Principles for Striking Gold

By Mike Schlappi, MBA

I t was the day of our school football team's championship game against our archrivals. As quarterback of the team, I felt 10-feet tall, excited, and ready to go.

En route to the game, my adrenaline pumping, I could hardly wait to pick up my friend so we could go together to this championship game. I rapped on the door of his home as I had done dozens of times before.

"Come on in," my friend called from the back bedroom. I sauntered around at first, then impatiently sat on the edge of the bed waiting for him to finish getting dressed. My friend's father was a policeman and I noticed his off-duty pistol on the night stand. Intrigued, I picked it up, thinking how heavy it felt in my hand. My friend came into the room and saw me holding his father's revolver. He reached over, took it from my hands, and unsnapped the leather cover. Without speaking, he flipped open the cylinder. I watched, transfixed, as he let the bullets fall harmlessly on the bed. One, two, three, four … five. They looked cool, all silver and sleek.

Believing the gun was empty, my friend started playing around with it. Then he innocently pointed it at my chest and pulled the trigger. The remaining .38 caliber bullet tore a massive hole through my shirt and ripped into my chest. I plummeted back against the headboard of the bed. My body convulsed violently while my mind struggled to comprehend what was happening. The bullet brushed past my heart then slammed into my backbone. I remember I could feel my collapsing lung fill with blood. Then I reached down with my right hand and I grasped my thigh. That action confirmed my greatest fear — there was no feeling at all from the contact my hand had made on the outside of my leg. The bullet left me paralyzed from the waist down.

That agonizing split-second event changed my life. It would be months and years before my family and I would experience its full impact. Fortunately, it set me on a course of destiny that contained blessings and promises I could never have had otherwise.

Attitude Therapy

I received a lot of physical and occupational therapy following my accident. Though I felt grateful for it, my greatest therapy actually came from the therapy I gave myself. I began calling it Attitude Therapy, which doesn't fall under any of the occupational or physical or speech or recreational therapy categories. Attitude Therapy seeks recovery "from the inside out." That means each of us, from time to time, needs to sculpt, change, or reframe the way we think. Regardless of how much help we receive from others, the greatest therapy exists in our minds — what we convince ourselves to do and to become. Speaking from the vantage point of a wheelchair, I realized I didn't need to hold back. We live by learning to relish the challenge of each new day to keep us going.

Here's how the idea of attitude therapy first came to me. When I was 16, I went with my family and a friend Roger

Dayton to Deer Creek Reservoir in Utah to water-ski for the day. After the others had taken their turns skiing, I wanted mine. So I put on a life jacket and flipped over the edge of the boat into the water. All I had to use for skis was a round yellow plywood board that Roger had brought along. So I pulled myself onto this board, grabbed a hold of the rope, and signaled for my dad to open up the throttle.

As he took off at full speed, I hung on for dear life. Even though the water kept hitting me in the face making it hard to see, I was having a blast. Then I noticed the people in our boat laughing wholeheartedly. At first, I thought one of my sisters, Julie or Collette, had told a joke, but I remembered neither one was that humorous. Immediately after, Dad swung the boat around and headed for shore.

By this time I felt self-conscious, thinking my legs were flipping around giving everyone a good laugh. I wondered if I looked like a fallen Superman. Just then, I glanced behind me to see that the water had pushed my swimsuit completely off my atrophied legs. I had been skiing in my birthday suit! I quickly slid off the board into the cover of the water and let go of the rope, then waited for Dad to pick me up.

I felt mortified, to be sure, but while I bobbed up and down in the lake, I realized this moment was much like my accident. I couldn't help what had happened to me, but my attitude could determine how I responded to it. I could either laugh and enjoy the humor of the moment, or sulk and get upset with how the others were acting. It was a great "wake up" call for me and proved to be the genesis of my Attitude Therapy business.

Paralympic Athlete

At the ripe old age of 25, I loved playing basketball as much as I did when I had been a star school athlete. I had become quite good at it, too. Though dribbling behind my wheelchair was more difficult than dribbling behind my back, I learned to do it well — along with skills like sinking baskets from a seated position and maneuvering around the court on wheels rather than in sneakers.

So knowing that we will certainly miss 100% of the shots we don't take, I decided to try out for the U.S. Paralympic basketball team. The second largest sporting event in the world, the Paralympic Games are a sister competition to the Olympics involving top athletes who have physical disabilities. I was fortunate to be the youngest athlete selected to play on the U.S. Paralympic basketball team in 1988 and have now competed in four Paralympic competitions — at Seoul, South Korea, in 1988; at Barcelona, Spain, in 1992; at Atlanta, Georgia, in 1996; most recently at Sydney, Australia, for the 2000 Games. (Unfortunately, I'm one of the oldest players on *this* team.) Though the results aren't known for the 2000 Games at the time of this writing, I'm honored to say our Paralympic team won medals during each of the other Games I competed in.

A twist of fate occurred during the 1992 Paralympics in Barcelona. Our team had capped the competition with a gold medal after a first-place win over the Netherlands. But shortly after returning home, the U.S. players received a letter stating we had to give our medals back or be barred from future competition for life.

The Paralympic officials had randomly selected one of our star players for a drug test, and he had tested positive. The drug was a painkiller that, while illegal at the time, is now legal for certain athletes to use in competition. Sending that medal back after having worked our hearts out to earn it was among the most difficult things I've ever done.

Yet, while it felt devastating at the time, I have used this negative event as a tool to dig even more deeply into resolve. I know that if life was always "rosy" and we never lost anything, we would fail to appreciate all the good things that happen. As an example of that, look what my good friend Dave Kiley did.

You see, it was Dave who had tested positive for using the illegal drug. After being stripped of our medals, he spent hundreds of hours trying to get the decision reversed. Though he didn't succeed, he went on to become the commissioner of the National Wheelchair Basketball Association (NWBA) so he could be a leader in this arena. Dave is a great example of using positive energy when something unexpected and undesirable happens. I'm proud to say Dave is again competing on our U.S. basketball team in the Sydney Paralympics.

Many people like Dave have demonstrated principles in their lives that I teach in my keynote presentations. I know they work. I call them the Bulletproof Principles for Success.

Bulletproof Principle Number One: Find your passion.

I believe people live to grow and to change rather than to merely exist. That's why it's so important for us to tackle life with a passion.

I first realized this principle right after I had been shot. At that time, my thinking lens was cloudy and I had to find a suitable "mental Windex" to regain clarity of vision. I was forced to dig deeply inside and create pressure for myself to just get up every morning. Learning to live with passion resulted from this time in my life; it became "mind over mattress" of the first order.

The opposite of living with passion is simply giving up — allowing others to push the "kill" button. Many people who die at age 75 actually stopped living at age 30.

Shortly after I was injured, I began competing in 26-mile marathons in my wheelchair. I loved the challenge. And although I fell behind at the beginning uphill portion of the race, I passed most of the runners on the downhill stretch. One day while competing in the Deseret News Marathon, I realized that participating in a race like this was much like life: people cheer us on at the beginning and thousands wait at the finish line to congratulate us. But the 24 difficult miles of asphalt in between is what really counts. In the final sum, our own passion determines our outcomes.

What passion keeps you going that extra distance?

Bulletproof Principle Number Two: Take responsibility for your attitudes.

Rather than project blame or allow the seeds of anger and discontent to enter your heart when something goes wrong, take control of your emotional response. I remember spending day after day blaming my friend for my paralysis, questioning *why* he shot me. Then I remember the day I decided to start taking responsibility for what happened. After all, I was the one who first played with the gun. This helped me shift my focus from past "victim thinking" toward future "victories." I reinforced that shift when I had that "bad butt day" trying to water-ski. I could have responded in a variety of ways — anger, upset, embarrassment. But I consciously chose to tap into the power of humor and laugh at myself. I still laugh heartily every time I tell this story.

Here's another example of taking responsibility, told through the experience of disabled pro golfer Casey Martin.

Because of Casey's extremely atrophied leg, a court judge ruled that he could ride a cart on the pro golf tour. As reported in the local paper (*The Daily Herald*, February 12, 1998, p. B1, Eugene, Oregon), "For Martin, the landmark ruling was not just a victory for him; it was a symbolic victory for all those with a disability who've been told they can't. 'I realized if I win,' Martin was quoted as saying, 'it would open the way. That's something to feel good about.'"

70

Martin not only excelled in his sport by winning a Professional Golf Association (PGA) tournament, but he invokes the Americans with Disabilities Act that allows him to compete on the professional level he has worked so hard to achieve. In this way and others, he has taken responsibility for his future.

What are you unwilling to take responsibility for? How can you change that?

Bulletproof Principle Number Three: Relish and accept adversity.

A year following my accident, I realized that people weren't being rude when they asked about my condition. They were simply curious. That's when I realized that the way I responded and carried myself would influence the way others would regard me. I wanted them to see me as a person with a personality rather than a paraplegic with an impairment. At this moment, I made a decision not only to accept my adversity but also to *relish* its acceptance.

What adversity in your life has made you a bitter person rather than a better person? How can you embrace adversity and turn it into something valuable for yourself?

Bulletproof Principle Number Four: Live with a service mentality.

From what I've seen, life is made up of takers and givers. Takers scavenge from society and givers contribute to it. As a 16-year-old, I decided not to accept pity, nor would I view myself as disabled. Rather, I was just a guy who had to dance in a wheelchair.

Still, I hesitated to ask girls to dance with me — why would they want to dance with a guy who couldn't really dance? Then at one particular school dance, a girl named Wendy invited me onto the floor. Before long, I was doing wheelies and goofing off right to the end of the song. She then caught me off-guard by inviting me to dance the next song — this time a slow dance. Neither of us knew what to do, so with an air of giving, she got down on her knees next to my chair. Now the pressure was on me to decide what to do next and I was sweating bullets (pardon the pun). Feeling awkward, I started patting her on the head to the beat of the music. But before long, she comfortably sat on my lap so we could coast around in each other's arms. With this thoughtful action, Wendy demonstrated what giving is all about and I learned to get out of my corner and flirt with change —to do something different.

Living with a service mentality makes a great difference … to others and to yourself. How can you strengthen that part of your life?

Bulletproof Principle Number Five: Never Give Up!

It's interesting that, when people speak to me, they are often consumed with questions about my injury, as if my disability was the only difficulty I had to contend with. They show surprise when I tell them that, just like them, I deal with all types of difficulties. Depression can set in when a business deal goes sour; anger can erupt when others don't meet my expectations, and so on. Some disabilities are simply more obvious than others. In fact, often the depth of the emotional and spiritual disabilities a person experiences far exceed any physical disability I might have.

What inner disabilities do you harbor? Have certain weaknesses become part of the baggage you carry around in an imaginary fanny pack? Do you take out your weaknesses and display them when it's convenient, then quietly tuck them out of sight when it isn't?

Hopelessness and failure can be the greatest disabilities. Hope and success, on the other hand, breed upon themselves. They allow you to enjoy a life of accomplishments, self-fulfillment, and peace.

Never give up, for personal change is always a possibility. By adopting these bulletproof principles, you share your light with the world.

> *"If we resist change, we'll fail,*
> *if we accept change, we'll survive,*
> *and if we create change, we'll succeed."*
> *– Anonymous*

* * * * *

Mike Schlappi, MBA, CSP
Draper, Utah

Mike Schlappi has looked adversity in the face and taught himself – and thousands of others – both how to change and how to *relish* life's changes. Now a popular keynote speaker and author, he promotes his ideas through his business Attitude Therapy.

Also a world-class wheelchair athlete, Mike is the only athlete to participate in the past four Paralympic Games as a gold-medal-winning member of the U.S. Wheelchair Basketball Team. He is on the Board of Trustees for the 2002 Olympic and Paralympic Games in Salt Lake City, and was recently honored by the state of Utah as one of its top 50 athletes for the past century. Mike founded the Wheelchair Sports Foundation, which provides sports and recreation for disabled athletes.

Born and raised in Utah, Mike earned his Bachelor of Science degree at Brigham Young University and his MBA at Arizona State University. The author of *Bulletproof Principles for Striking Gold,* Mike's story was featured in the national award-winning video *If You Can't Stand Up, Stand Out.* Mike is a member of the National Speakers Association.

Contact Information:
Mike Schlappi, MBA, CSP
Mike Schlappi Communications
641 East Pheasant Haven Court • Draper, UT 84020
Phone: 801-553-MIKE(6453)
Email: mike@mikeschlappi.com
Website: www.mikeschlappi.com

CHAPTER 6

Why Seemingly Smart People Do Stupid Things

By Susan Carnahan

Vivacious. Dynamic. Entertaining. Effective. These are just the initial words that begin to describe **Susan Carnahan**. There is a more important word that serves as a foundation for these, however. That word is "smart." She is smart in the lessons she delivers. She is smart in the way she delivers her messages. It makes for an inspiring combination; smart and effective.   – VO

* * * * *

Winners believe in their worth
in advance of their performance.
– Dennis Waitley

Why Seemingly Smart People Do Stupid Things

Lessons for Gaining
Greater Control of Your Life

BY SUSAN CARNAHAN

W e all make them! They are inevitable. In fact, at the time you make a mistake, it *isn't* one; mistakes aren't mistakes until after the fact. But true success lies in recognizing self-defeating behavior and replacing it with life-affirming action.

This chapter highlights four of life's dumbest mistakes smart people make, and shows you practical ways of thinking, feeling and acting to stop them in their tracks. The four are:

- Near-Sightedness
- Procrastination
- Perfectionism
- The Superhuman Syndrome

Mistake # 1 — Near-sightedness

A Far Side Cartoon reads: *Encumbered by a low self-image, Bob takes a job as a speed bump.* Aren't there times when we feel we have not lived up to our full potential?

Go back ten years. How old were you? Where were you living? How were you earning a living? What issues were consuming your time and energy? What physical shape were you in? How was your mental health?

Contrast that to your current lifestyle. Where do you now reside? How are you making a living today? What issues exhaust most of your time and energy? How is your physical and mental health today compared with ten years ago?

I call this the "WOW" assignment because you're likely thinking, "Wow, I've come a long way in ten years. This feels great." Or you may be thinking, "Wow, where have I been for the last ten years?" I believe the latter reaction occurs more often than the former one because we fail to envision our futures. Often in our busy-ness, we don't take time to stop and assess where we have been, where we are and, most importantly, where we see ourselves ten years down the road.

So what do you *really* want to be when you grow up, anyway? Isn't that life's million-dollar question? I can't predict where you will be ten years from now, but I know you will arrive there before you turn around and blink.

Avoiding Near-Sightedness

The road to personal excellence does not begin with a book or a seminar; it begins in your head. It begins with your thoughts. And as the saying goes — *you can only achieve what you can conceive and then believe.* For example, if you started working at the age of 12, 13, or 14, you probably worked illegally, getting paid "under the table." Do you remember thinking, "Someday, I'm going to earn minimum wage"? You had stars in your eyes. Then, when you were making minimum wage, you had to raise the bar and dared to imagine making $30,000 a year — someday. Once achieved, you raised your sights again: $50,000 a year, $80,000 a year, $100,000 a year.

Are you with me? If you can't conceive of earning a six-digit income, it will likely never happen. In fact, the *Law of Expectations* says that whatever we expect with confidence becomes our own self-fulfilling prophecy. That means people who enjoy high levels of success continually talk *to* and *about* themselves as though they expect great things in their lives. You *can* make your dreams happen, goal-by-goal, step-by-step. The power is within you; the plan to succeed begins in your mind.

If you wander through life humming *What's It All About, Alfie* and feel stuck, then here's a tip. Break your plans down into manageable chunks. Ask yourself, "Where do I hope to be three years from now?" Three-year increments don't seem so overwhelming; they actually feel manageable. And three years from now, if you aren't enjoying where you are at, you haven't lost time. Rather, you've gained experience. This critical tool builds the confidence you need to survive and thrive in this world.

Tools to Use

"Nothing much happens without a dream. For something really great to happen, it takes a really great dream."
– Anonymous

Begin with the dream. Take the roof off the building where you sit and tell yourself the sky is the limit. And if that's the beginning of dreaming, then ask yourself this:

- If money is no object, what type of home would you live in ten years from now?

- If location were no object, where in this world would you like to live ten years from now?

- If education were no object, what would you like to do for a living in ten years?

- If failing were no object and the next dream you pursued would accomplish results beyond your wildest imagination, what path would you walk on? (And the next time you diet, you will never, ever gain the weight back again!)

In a Peanuts cartoon, Charlie Brown is target practicing with a bow and arrow. He pulls the bowstring back as hard as he can, then lets the arrow fly. It finally sticks in the center of a fence post. Charlie Brown races up to the arrow, pulls out a giant crayon, and draws a big ole' bulls eye around it. Lucy walks by, looks at the arrow, and says, "That's not how you target practice, Charlie Brown. You draw the target first and then you shoot the arrow." Charlie Brown says, "I know that Lucy, but if you do it my way, you never miss!" Perhaps you are afraid to visualize your ten-year target because there is a chance you may not succeed, so you never start on the path in the first place. If that's true, then read on about Mistake #2.

Mistake #2 — Procrastination

Are you the one who put the "pro" in the word procrastination? Then you are one of many people who go through life "but" first, saying, "But first, I think I'll do this. But I would rather do that first." It's easy to put off today what should have been done yesterday.

Would you not accomplish what you do without deadlines? Doesn't each deadline actually create a negative form of energy called stress that propels you so you end up going through life backward instead of forward? Do you *react* to life instead of approaching it proactively? Do you need to draw the target first or you'll never shoot the arrow? These questions identify the procrastinators in the crowd.

Avoiding Procrastination

Procrastinators experience an extreme fear of failing. Think about this: if you put something off until the last minute, you never test your true talents, so you never know if you succeed or fail. All you can measure is your ability to throw things together at the last minute.

Instead, follow Nike's motto … and just do it! Remember the daughter who turned to her mom and said, "I think I'll go back to school and become a doctor." Her mother said, "A doctor! Dear, by the time you're a doctor, you'll be over 50." The daughter replied, "I'll be over 50 anyway, whether I'm a doctor or not."

Tools to Use

Find your own ways to liberate yourself from compulsive procrastination. Some examples are:

- Set a kitchen timer and tell yourself you will work for 15 minutes on the project you're avoiding.

- When the timer rings, reward yourself. Ice cream works!

- Break the project into a series of "do-able" steps. Create a one-month plan, then four one-week plans, then seven one-day plans. Soon you're on your way to making it happen through your talents and strengths.

Mistake #3 — Perfectionism

Do you have the "perfect" point of view? Perfectionists may deny it but they're easy to identify because they live by the motto: *There are three ways to do things: the right way, the wrong way, and my way.*

Because of the belief that "if I want something done right, I have to do it myself," a perfectionist's most difficult task is delegation. Indeed, delegation makes life more enjoyable by giving us time to do the things we *want* to do ... not the things we *have* to do. Delegating also becomes a great compliment because it says, "I trust you." And trust is the foundation of all relationships. Did you notice that when you don't trust someone, you withhold information? And without information, a relationship becomes stale and dies.

A popular definition of perfectionism states: "A perfectionist is someone who takes great pains and then gives them to everyone else." So if your partner is driving the car, what gives you the right to tell him or her where to park? If your friend has decided to take a different job, what gives you the right to tell her she's wrong? If your spouse is pruning the bushes, what gives you the right to bark instructions? Perfectionism leads to nagging that leads to a communication breakdown and unsatisfying relationships.

Avoiding Perfectionism

Practice recognizing when you are in a destructive habit and consciously correct it. Catching yourself "in the act" can be the biggest challenge of all!

When you suffer from perfectionism, three ugly consequences could happen:

1. You may die earlier than most because you're exhausted doing everything yourself.

2. You overlook innovative ways to do things because you are mentally stuck in a rut. My father used to insist we mow the lawn in the same direction, in the same tire tracks, each and every time. Today we have learned that mowing in the same direction every time actually harms the grass. By insisting something be done your way, you tend to overlook possible shortcuts, creative solutions, and new perspectives on old problems.

3. The people who surround you tend to have low self-esteem, whether it's your teammates at work, your partner at home, or your children. Keep in mind that we can't *give* other people confidence. But we can rob them of the opportunity to earn it themselves by not delegating.

Jennifer James once wrote, "Perfectionism is just a fancy word for a nag." The next time you hear your critical voice correcting someone, ask yourself, "Where is it written it has to be done this way?" And the next time you hear yourself say, "You didn't do it right," rephrase it and say, "You didn't do it *my way*." It's more honest.

Tools to Use

Try on these ideas for practice:

- Quickly straighten your desk rather than stopping to be thorough on each item.

- Leave a voice mail message without re-recording it several times.

- Let the kids load the dishwasher and your partner clean the house to meet *their* standards, not yours.

- Leave the house without making your bed.

Mistake #4 — The Superhero Syndrome

It's time to retire the cape. Do you know any rescuers? I once met the greatest rescuers on earth, a couple married for 65 years. The wife, 83, and her husband, 79, both worry about getting older. Who would take care of them should the need arise?

They are counting on the loyalty of their youngest son who just turned 40. He moved out of their home for the very first time — this year. But he moved next door to his parents' house into a home they bought for him. That way, his mother could go over every morning to make his breakfast, clean his house, and do his laundry. They also worry about what would become of their son if they passed away because "he needs us so much."

The tragedy in this story isn't the son; it's the parents. What would they do if their son left first … for they need him so much? Without him, how then would they measure their worth in this world?

The person who is overly responsible for others and their actions — the one who rescues loved ones from having to account for themselves and their reaction to situations — causes the people around them to be irresponsible. Here is the irony: irresponsible people don't mind! It's an easy way to go through life without failing, without criticism, but also without the necessary experiences to grow. Sometimes, we must let people fail so they can make mistakes, learn from them, and gain self-esteem.

Perhaps those who are constantly rescued in this world are the ones who have a hard time with delegation. Have you ever tried to delegate work to someone who responds with, "That's not in my job description?" It may not be their reluctance to help or learn new skills or add accomplishments to their resume. Most likely, it's their fear of failing. They feel paralyzed because they have seldom failed; they have always been rescued instead.

Avoiding The Superhero Syndrome

It is the awesome responsibility of leaders, managers and parents to create an environment that says, "It's OK to fail." The next time you make a mistake, confess it in public. Discuss it and help others learn from it, too. American chroniclers could re-write history if only President William Clinton had learned from this valuable lesson in life.

Tools to Use

Find your own ways to liberate yourself from the Superhero Syndrome. Some examples might be:

- Say the word "no" at least twice this week to a request for your involvement.

- Let others solve their own problems this week.

- Take the phone off the hook all weekend long.

- Compliment someone ... delegate a task or two.

- Empower others ... ask them for help!

Your Wake-Up Call

All four of these mistakes share one common denominator — the fear of failing, which, ironically, is the fear of making a mistake. Now we come full circle.

Consider what your life would be like if your fear of failure took complete control of your actions. You'd never get married or develop relationships — they might not last. You'd never ask for a raise — you might get turned down. You'd never offer a suggestion — it could get voted down.

Truly successful people wouldn't change one single, solitary thing in their past because their experiences have provided the wisdom and character upon which they have built their successes. This includes failed marriages, devastating illnesses, losses of loved ones, even failures to invest in the latest high-tech stock! Some people ask, "Is there life after death?" when the question should be, "Is there life *before* death?"

Helen Keller said, "Security is mostly superstition. It does not exist in nature, nor do children experience it. Life is either a daring adventure or nothing."

Dare to learn from your mistakes.

*   *   *   *   *

Susan Carnahan
Monument, Colorado

 Voted *Consummate Speaker of the Year 2000*, Susan Carnahan has become known for delivering humorous, content-driven messages that motivate people to make long-term, meaningful changes in their personal and professional lives. Since 1987, Susan has challenged corporate leaders and their employees across the United States and Canada to achieve higher levels of productivity by focusing on change from the inside out.

Using her experience in broadcasting, banking, law and parenting, Susan addresses more than 150,000 business professionals a year. Audiences relate to her powerful stories that illustrate why people prefer to stay stuck in routines, rather than risk new ways of thinking, communicating and leading. They come away rediscovering the joy of change and reaching for higher performance standards.

Born and raised in Colorado, Susan attended Mesa College in Grand Junction, Colorado and Northern Arizona University in Flagstaff. She has appeared on CNN Live on gender communication skills and has written several audio and video programs including *What's Sex Got To Do With It, Lessons In Leadership, Leadership And Supervisory Skills For Women*, and *Self-Empowerment For Women*. Susan and Ron, her husband of over 30 years, have 2 adult children, a horse named Dakota, and a shepherd-lab dog named Durango.

Contact Information:
Carnahan Presents!
18625 Wethersfield Drive • Monument, CO 80132
Phone: 719-481-8904
FAX: 719-488-8376
www.carnahanpresents.com
susancarnahan@carnahanpresents.com

PART TWO

Motivating and Leading Others

CHAPTER 7

Going Up? Take the Team With You!

BY DOUG CARTLAND

Doug Cartland has heart. When he speaks, he speaks from the heart. He shares his message with intensity, with passion and with conviction. But what magnifies this and enhances his ability to impart his message is that he has an unparalleled ability to listen with his heart also. The ability to understand and then deliver makes him a true motivator.– VO

*   *   *   *   *

Be faithful to that which exists
nowhere but in yourself.
– Andre Gide

Going Up?
Take the Team
With You!

By Doug Cartland

I was the worst high school cross country runner in the history of mankind. I was a little speck of a person as a freshman — 4' 11" and 86 pounds. Severe scoliosis left me with a crooked back and a somewhat bulging chest. My chest was such that a bully stood next to me in the school lunch line one day and referred to me as the "kid with one tit." True.

My first race ended with my teammates (already back in their sweats, sipping Mountain Dew) screaming for me to sprint the final 100 yards or so. Well, I promise you reader, my heart was sprinting, but my legs were not moving very fast. When I finished, the thrill of being done was quickly overwhelmed by the agony of the dry-heaves.

Given these facts, how popular do you think I was with the rest of the cross country team? If your answer is "not very," you're right.

Something strange happened, however, about half way through the season. Coach Gunderson (the head cross country coach) was addressing the team as we sat on bleachers near the cross country trail. He was talking about courage and effort and fortitude and all that good stuff coaches and leaders talk about when they want to motivate — the stuff that often goes through one ear and out the other. At one point he said, "If I ever see any one of you not running your very hardest in a race, I will come and personally take you off the cross country course." Still pretty standard fare. But then he stopped for a moment and said, "I know one guy I will never have to pull from a cross country course, ever." And he walked over, took his finger, tapped me on the knee and said, "This guy right here."

I was shocked. Two things happened in that moment. First, it was a rapture for me — I would have sworn I had seen God right then. I had never felt that way in my life. All of the shackles of self-loathing fell away for a moment and all was right with the world.

Those feelings, of course, were temporary but the second thing that happened was not. I, for the very first time, became part of the team. From that day on, the team accepted me as one of them. I never became a great cross country runner — not that year, not ever. But the team, in that moment, saw and began to appreciate my value.

Coach Gunderson had simply done a leader's job. He had seen beyond my physical stature. He had looked beneath my skin and found my heart, and in my heart what I had to offer to the team.

Contrary to popular belief, the key to creating a team is NOT better communication, or having the same vision, or cooperation, or good chemistry. The foundation of a team goes much deeper than that. The basis for teamwork is genuine respect for each other and what each other brings to the table — a respect that goes beyond stature, beyond gender, beyond race, beyond economic status, even beyond ideologies and disagreements. With this respect COMES communication, shared vision, cooperation, good chemistry and, ultimately, team success. Teambuilding, then, is the nurturing and facilitating of that respect.

I'm going to define respect, but, before I do, let me be clear about what I am NOT talking about. First, I am not talking about agreement. If we as leaders are looking for everybody on the team to agree perfectly, our efforts will be futile and the team will fail. Nobody has the whole answer, thus we all have a portion of the answer at best. A passage in the Bible says we "see in part." I can buy that. None of us can know everything about anything, thus we rely on the views of others where we fall short. This creates the need for a team.

The United States of America is built on disagreement — it was bricked right into the Constitution with our freedoms of speech and religion, etc. If we all agreed, the freedoms would not be necessary. The key is to live with each other, paying attention to our disagreements in an effort to learn from each other, but to not be overwhelmed and divided by them. In our collective contributions lie our best answers and solutions.

If you want a place that purports to have no disagreements then join a religious cult — I did for almost ten years. Of course, even there, the disagreements exist. They are just quashed by men and women in authority, and then ultimately by you because you conform out of your longing to be accepted. It is amazing what we will agree with when acceptance is the reward. True in teenage gangs. True in cults. True in business meetings too.

The cult example brings me to the second thing that respect is NOT. Respect is NOT tolerance. When I was in the cult we were often accused of being intolerant. We certainly were that, but the genuine respect that creates a team environment and produces a positive intelligent direction for a group, goes well beyond tolerance.

Often political, business and community leaders encourage tolerance. Are we really looking for a society, or community, or business, or organization that thrives on tolerance? You cannot build with tolerance. Tolerance is "live and let live." Tolerance is arrogant. What do you mean you TOLERATE me?!

We tolerate whites, we tolerate blacks, we tolerate gays, we tolerate men, we tolerate women, we tolerate our children, we tolerate our husbands and wives! We say, "It's all right if he's gay as long as he doesn't come into my store!" Or, "It's all right if he's Hispanic as long as he doesn't live on my block!" We can exist separately and tolerate. We can tolerate and not build a thing. Ask a husband and wife what kind of marriage they're building if they're at the point where they're just tolerating each other. Ask a business team, or sports team, or community team what kind of environment they have if their relationships have been reduced to tolerance. I'll tell you one thing they don't have — they don't have a team.

Now, genuine respect IS recognizing the gifts and value in others and utilizing those gifts and that value. It's as simple as that. If the bad news is that everybody "sees in part," then the good news is that everybody "sees in part!" So everyone sees! Everyone has a contribution. In one area that contribution may be small, but in another it will be much larger.

So how does a leader utilize everybody's contributions? The Reverend Jesse Jackson calls it "inclusion." How do we include? By including!

My son, Tim, was eight years old playing on a t-ball team that I helped coach. Tim was one of the better players and thus fairly popular with the team. Brett was another boy on the team and was a terrible baseball player. Of course, at that age his lack of athleticism led other boys to not want to include him.

94

One night, on the way to our game, I asked Tim about Brett. He agreed that most of the kids ignored Brett and that he was often left alone or playing catch with one of the coaches. Then I asked Tim to do something that was anathema to any eight year old.

"Tim?" I began. "How would you feel if you were in Brett's shoes?"

"Not very good, I guess," he replied.

"What would happen," I was treading lightly, "If you partnered with Brett for warm-ups tonight?"

Without hesitation, to my pleasant surprise, he said, "Okay." The simplicity of inclusion is to include!! No hesitation! No complicated questions about the potential political or social ramifications! No ego! A simple decision to include.

Tim warmed up with Brett that night and a very strange thing began to happen. The others began to warm up to Brett. Tim, one of the popular kids, reached out and the others began to respond.

I will finish this illustration with a story that is so amazing in its profound coincidence that I couldn't make it up if I tried. In our last game of the season, it was the bottom of the last inning, there were two out, we were ahead by one and the opposing team had a runner on second. Brett was playing catcher (generally the safest place to put a poor player in t-ball).

The hitter drove a base-hit to left field. Our left-fielder came up with the ball as the runner rounded third. I figured we'd soon have a tie game. Our left-fielder stepped up and threw the ball home. Brett did not move the mitt dangling at his side. The ball hit the glove (I'm not kidding), stuck in it, the runner ran into Brett and the ball and was out. We won the game. All of our players ran to Brett, slapped him on the head and hoisted him in the air, shouting and cheering him for getting the final out. It was a scene that that young man will never forget — nor

I. All because one popular boy — a leader — chose to include one that seemed to have no place. You include by including.

Leadership is the ability to unify a team, motivate it and head it in an intelligent direction. It's the ability to interpret the gifts and abilities of those with you to best utilize them. And it is realizing that every motivated member of the team has a contribution to make no matter how small it may seem.

Leadership is also realizing that the best success is not the success you achieve on your own, but the success you experience together. Bringing EVERYONE to the finish line, as one, should be the goal of any leader.

Ray Eliot was the legendary football coach at the University of Illinois from 1942 through 1959. In 1946 he had many players return from World War Two who had had great potential before they left. Some were as old as 24 or 25 when they returned; a few were even married with kids. Many had been officers in the war, while others spent time in prisoner of war camps. They had been to hell and back. They were heroes.

Now these war veterans had to mesh with college kids who knew nothing of war and had established positions for themselves while the veterans were away. As I wrote in my book about Eliot, "It was a minefield of egos and emotions, of psyches and spirit." Even so, the media had Illinois winning a Big 10 championship — and some a National Championship — before the season even began.

The Illini started by playing poorly in a 33-7 win over Pittsburgh. They were then hammered by Notre Dame, 26-6. Eliot was perplexed. He decided to change his approach and became, for a brief time, a taskmaster. The team seemed to respond by whipping Purdue the next week 43-7. But then the wheels fell off in a 14-7 loss to Indiana.

The leader, Eliot, was depressed and confused. Expectations were large for this group of men, but he had not been able to find the key to unlock the door of success. Petitions were circulating around the Champaign-Urbana campus demanding he be fired. The frustration was mounting. He began to question his own abilities and went to Athletic Director Doug Mills, offering his resignation, which Mills promptly rejected.

Eliot thought hard about the situation. Gradually he began to realize what he was dealing with. He was treating the veterans like boys and not like the men they had become. For their part, the veterans came back from the war hard, self-sufficient and cocky, feeling like they really didn't need a coach or anybody else.

Eliot decided it was his place to make the first move. He called a meeting with his players and respectfully listened to their complaints. To tell the truth, not many of their ideas had much merit, but the players appreciated being listened to. Eliot's show of genuine, heartfelt respect opened up the lines of communication. That, in turn, earned Eliot the right to show them what they were doing wrong. He demonstrated to his players how they were not playing as a team — they were all out there doing their own thing. Now THEY listened and decided he was right. Eliot and his players carried that mutual respect — from coach to player, from player to coach, from player to player — through the rest of that wonderful, magical season.

I wish I had room here to go through all the details with you, but they rolled off seven wins in a row from that day, including a 45-14 trouncing of previously unbeaten UCLA in the Rose Bowl after winning the Big 10 Championship!

Other coaches had the same problems with returning veterans (though Illinois had more returning than anybody), but nobody had the same results as Ray Eliot. Other teams fell apart under the strain — none but Illinois reached its potential.

Team respect begins with the leader's respect for those under her/him. This is the first step to the leader facilitating respect among them and creating a team.

I have had the privilege of talking to many great educators over the years. There are different philosophies and personalities that work with students. But the one common thread that runs through all successful educational approaches is the educator's respect for the people being educated. When a student, or an athlete, or an employee knows that you, the leader, respect them, they open themselves up much more readily to your criticism and direction because they trust that you have their, and the team's, best interest at heart.

One of the most beautiful things to watch at a high school is a play or musical because it brings together kids from a multitude of backgrounds as one, and they create art. It is sometimes kind of rough around the edges, but it is art nonetheless. Athletes, "nerds," cheerleaders, poor students, good students, different races, all classes, all religions, both genders, pulling together and celebrating each other's success and the success of the team.

This is THE global issue isn't it? Whether it's the world, a nation, a large corporation, a small organization, an athletic team or a school play, seeing beneath the surface and finding people's gifts and value is the key. There can be no unity, no team, without this genuine respect. It negates racism or sexism or any other "ism" because we look below the surface. This is the leader's job — to find the gifts in the hearts of men and women and utilize them.

"Seeds of Peace" is an organization that brings together 12 to 15 year old kids from Israel and Palestinian countries. These hated enemies get together in a camp in Maine for three weeks during the summer. They laugh with each other, cry with each other, play sports, discuss issues and eat together — all for one reason: To put a face on the enemy. And it works. These kids discover for themselves the gifts in the people they were taught to despise. They go in as hated enemies and leave as friends. They do not come out necessarily AGREED on issues, but they come out agreeing that each point of view is worthy of respect. And they see that, contrary to what they have been taught, each individual has value and something valuable to offer.

Now, if these kids can come across an ocean to work through their differences, can we as leaders walk across a hallway, or reach our hands across a boardroom table to nurture and facilitate a unity and oneness born of genuine mutual respect that will head our business or organization in a positive, intelligent direction? Team success demands it.

* * * * *

Doug Cartland
Harvard, Illinois

Thousands of people and hundreds of organizations have been moved and re-energized by Doug and his message, whether through his speaking, his books or his award winning radio show, "Winning."

Featured on radio stations and in newspapers throughout the Midwest, Doug is different. His mixture of passion, humor and story-telling challenges his listeners in a most palatable way. He survived a religious cult for ten years and went on to become a successful business leader, community organizer, coach and father; all of which give him deep insights into teamwork, teambuilding and leadership.

If you question his zeal, his willingness to be different, and to go the distance, just ask him about his fundraising trip on a lawn tractor at seven miles per hour around all of Lake Michigan!! Just ask...he'll tell you all-l-l-l about it....

Contact Information:
Doug Cartland
P.O. Box 753 • Harvard, IL 60033
Phone: (815) 943-7360
Fax: (815) 943-5120
E-mail: doug@dougcartland.com
Web Site: www.dougcartland.com

CHAPTER 8

The Importance of Mission in Management

By Kevin Lust

Kevin Lust is a big man with the potential to intimidate without even trying … except for one thing … the biggest parts about Kevin are his heart and his smile! Kevin is compelling and articulate, but his message is fueled with a passion and compassion that are so much a part of him that he profoundly touches everyone he meets, and everyone he presents to.   – VO

* * * * *

The greater thing in this world
is not so much where we stand as in
what direction we are going.
– Oliver Wendell Holmes

The Importance of Mission in Management

By Kevin Lust

M uch has been made in recent years of the importance of mission in organizational success. Great numbers of companies, small businesses, charitable groups, and even individuals have gone to extraordinary lengths to create, define, and redefine lengthy, all-encompassing, politically correct "Statements of Mission." Most of them have wasted their time.

A Mission That Works

Gather any group of business people in a room, ask for a show of hands on how many work for a company that has a mission statement, and you'll feel a stiff breeze as nearly every arm starts waving. Ask how many have actually read it, and you'll feel hardly a stir. Ask how many read it every day, and the room will be as still as a May morning.

Those hands stay quiet because missions are decided, re-corded, engraved on a plaque for the foyer, and then never referred to again. Most mission statements aren't statements at all. After contributions, clarifications, additions, expansions, committee approvals, and board reviews, simple statements of organizational purpose evolve into "mission paragraphs" or "mission couple-of-pages" or even "mission handbooks" (Volumes I & II). They end up looking like Dilbert-creator Scott Adams' definition of mission statements: long, awkward sentences demonstrating management's inability to think clearly. And long, awkward sentences serve no purpose.

The mission that works is quite simple. It is a few words defining the fundamental purpose of the organization or individual, not much more. For example, John Carver cites the mission of the Ohio State Board of Education and the Ohio Department of Education as, "Literate Ohio Citizens." Perfect. While the organization's formal document continues to define specific outputs that support its fundamental purpose, no more needs to be said. Any employee of those institutions can use those three words as a fountain of motivation, a source of empowerment, or a powerful decision-making tool.

More than anything, the mission statement is fundamentally what you DO. Be careful, that's not just what you do. It is what you DO. Ask people who work for a telephone company what they do and most will say this: they provide telephone service. And that's a correct, appropriate answer. It is not the right answer, however, to the real question: what does the phone company DO?

What the phone company DOES is allow every business in existence today to do business in the way they do business. Wouldn't it be a lot harder to do your work if it weren't for the telephone? You might be thinking, "No, I'd get a lot more work done if it wasn't for the darn phone," but that is not true. You wouldn't even *have* the work if you didn't have telephones. Can you imagine one of your customers saying, "I'll call you with my order," and you replying, "Nope, sorry, no phones here, but we are seriously considering trying that new electricity thing."

What the phone company also DOES is allow friends and family members the opportunity to stay in touch with one another, though they may be hundreds or thousands of miles apart. Did you call your Mom on Mother's Day? With the touch of three buttons, 911, the phone company also allows family or neighbors of a heart attack victim or a choking baby or someone in a car crash to call for emergency help. That's what the phone company DOES; therefore, that's what its mission is.

To distill all that information into a few simple words is no small task, but saying "we allow people to communicate no matter how far apart they are" provides a good start. Too simple? Well, contrast that statement with the two-column, fourteen-part, polysyllabic mission statements you've seen, and then decide which one works.

This type of mission demonstrates its real power through its variety of uses: motivator, decision-maker, disciplinary device. The effective mission serves the accomplished manager or individual as a universal tool, sort of the "duct tape" of success.

A Mission That Motivates

As a motivator, awareness of a stated mission literally can get people out of bed in the morning. At the phone company, members of the line crew climb 40-foot poles in 100° summer heat and crawl into manholes in 10° winter weather. Motivation might not be apparent to them on those days. But with a mission in front of them — remembering that climbing that pole today might save someone's life tomorrow — the task becomes a powerful, if not even positive, experience.

The old line says there are two types of people in the world: those who wake up in the morning singing "Good morning, Lord!" and those who crawl out of bed croaking "Good Lord, it's morning." Consider the bank teller who knows he's keeping peoples' money secure, the quick-lube oil change technician who knows she's helping peoples' cars last longer, the baker at the doughnut shop who knows he's getting his customers' mornings off to a cheerful (if fattening) start. All of these workers face the day with a little extra energy and a lot more purpose when they know their mission.

Lest you doubt the power of mission as a motivator, consider the multitudes of people who serve willingly and gladly in jobs that lack what many consider the primary motivator — money. Schoolteachers, drug abuse counselors, zookeepers, historians — all could have made more money if they'd gone into the computer field. But they wouldn't be doing what they felt they were there to DO. Money, benefits, status, fame, all fall short when compared to the value of DOING their job. If you have a poor performer on your team or lack energy yourself, call attention to the end product of your labor — and the people affected by it — and you'll see a big change in effort.

Remember that developing your mission doesn't have to be some big, grand, save-the-planet type adventure. One group said, "It's hard for us to have a compelling mission based on what we do." They work for a company that makes ketchup packets, like the ones you get with your french fries in your to-go order at Burgerland. They said, "What's our mission — a world in which everyone has ketchup packets?" Well, yeah! If you like ketchup, think about how much you enjoy slathering it on a hot order of fries. If you sit in your car when you eat them, you are not likely to have a spare bottle of ketchup in the console next to the gum wrappers, 63 cents in nickels and pennies, and old deposit slips from the bank. So people who make ketchup packets allow you to enjoy your meal more. It's what they DO.

A Mission That Makes Decisions

This tip about mission makes every choice you face automatically easier from this day forward. You can correctly make any decision — whether it's where to invest your time or money, how to handle a customer complaint, when to start (or stop) a project, which report to finish — if you will only reference your mission before you decide. Here is the key question: "Is what I'm about to do going to move me closer to my mission or further away from it?"

When my wife and I first started dating, I lived in Chicago, Illinois, and she lived in Milwaukee, Wisconsin. Although long distance, the geography wasn't a big problem as it only took two hours to drive from my house to hers (which many people consider a short commute in Chicago). It wasn't a problem, that is, when we first started dating.

You see, the reason *why* I lived in Chicago was due to *where* I lived in Chicago: five blocks from Wrigley Field where the Chicago Cubs play baseball. I love baseball and I love the Cubs (no comments about those being mutually exclusive) and that's why I lived in Chicago. So when we first met in November and started dating, we had no conflicts. But when spring rolled around, things changed. Every weekend that the Cubs played at Wrigley, I faced a major decision: "Should I go to Milwaukee or go the game?" And then the question became: "How many times can I actually go to the game before I no longer have any reason to go to Milwaukee?!?"

Initially, I had a tough time answering that question because I had no sense of why I ought to do either one — no sense of how either would help me reach my mission — because I didn't *know* my mission. But once I did know, and once we decided to get married and spend the rest of our lives together, the choice between going to Milwaukee or going to the game became a snap. (And don't you dare say, "Go to the game!") Going to Milwaukee helped me reach my ultimate mission.

"Investment" Approach to Decision-Making

This approach works across the board in the decisions that challenge you.

Which of the 107 items on your to-do list should you tackle first? The one that moves you closest to your mission. Which project gets the biggest budget? The one that best accomplishes your mission. Where should a team devote most of its energy? To the activities that contribute the most to its mission.

Another way to clarify this is to consider the distinction between investments and expenditures. Investments have a return; they move you closer to your mission. Expenditures do not.

For example, put young children in a store (it doesn't matter what child or what store) and what happens? They quickly find something they want. They race to mom or dad, squealing, "I want this. I want this. I want this." And what are the first words out of the parent's mouth? (Okay, besides, "no.") "How much does it cost?" And the child says, "$20." The parent says, "It costs too much; put it back." So the child finds something else for $15 and then for $12 and $7 and $5, until finally mom or dad relents and the article goes home — an expenditure that quickly ends up in the land of toys played with once.

That initial "how much" question starts this unfortunate situation. If the primary decision-maker is cost, eventually you arrive at an amount that's acceptable. Consequently, if you have enough money, you can spend it on anything.

Unfortunately, people typically don't have enough money, or time, or resources, or help, or equipment, or inventory, or whatever. Thus, the decision of where to invest or spend what you *do* have becomes critical. To make this difficult question simple, don't ask how much something costs until you ask *why* you want it. If the why helps you reach your mission, then you're making an investment. If not, you're going the wrong way and making an expenditure. No one can afford a perpetual diet of expenditures without eventually going broke. Conversely, if you recognize a good investment, you almost always can afford it.

If the *why* is big enough, the *how* will come.

A Mission That Disciplines

Your mission becomes a great empowering and disciplinary device as well.

Once upon a time, there were enough managers and supervisors in the world that they could, and often did, micromanage employee activity. Suspicious supervisors asked what employees were working on, if they arrived at work on time, did they take more breaks than they should have. They didn't realize that this inherent lack of trust not only created deficient behaviors but was annoying on top of it all! But after wave upon wave of downsizing and rightsizing (or, as one guy said, capsizing) swept through middle management, a relentless thrust to "do more with less" began. Now, most managers hardly have time to monitor their own progress, let alone anyone else's.

If the "my-way-or-the-highway" style of management ever did work, it sure doesn't work today. Not only will people in today's workplace fail to respond when getting treated like misbehaving children, they will also leave the organization.

Your mission comes into play when you teach your team those two words mentioned earlier: investment and expenditure. Remember, investments move you closer to your mission and expenditures do not.

At any given moment, members of your team should be able to explain how the activity in which they're engaged is an investment that helps the organization move closer to its mission. If the activity isn't moving the team toward the mission, it becomes an expenditure. With education and reinforcement in the meaning of your mission, you can teach your team to make these decisions without you. That's called empowerment.

No Need to List Rules

Do you see how this allows you to be a more flexible, coaching-style leader?

The old-style supervisor listed rules to be followed: one fifteen-minute break in the morning and one in the afternoon; no personal phone calls; be at your work station at x:30 sharp. By contrast, the mission-based coach takes a situational approach and says, "Oh, you're in customer service and that last irate customer really upset you? Maybe a five-minute break from the phones will help you compose yourself so you can serve the next customer better." "Your child is sick at home and you're having trouble concentrating? Maybe a quick phone call to confirm her progress will help you get back to this vital project." "Coming in fifteen minutes late in the morning and leaving fifteen minutes later at night works better for your schedule? Great, that may help us with those last-minute customers who always seem to show up."

For every one of these examples, people can find fifteen reasons why they won't work, declaring, "People will take advantage of the breaks." So you show them how that's not consistent with the mission. "They'll make too many calls." Then you tell them how that impacts the work that needs to be done. "They'll come and go as they please!" Well, is that so awful — as long as the work is getting done? So move away from monitoring activities and start measuring results. You'll become a more effective manager and a better person.

This Mission Does Work

Take the time to identify your mission, both organizationally and personally. Teach it to those who work with you and share it with those close to you. Watch how it excites them and feel how it enthuses you. You're getting something done. And you know you're getting the *right* thing done because you've made your choices based on your mission. You are investing in it with your every action. You empower and discipline at the same time by recognizing different ways to achieve the same results. And you become focused, decisive, flexible, and a lot easier to live with.

You have a mission.

* * * * *

Kevin Lust, CSP
Springfield, Illinois

As a full time professional speaker and trainer since 1990, Kevin Lust has delivered nearly 1,500 presentations in 16 countries on four continents. Before founding The Lust Development Group, Kevin enjoyed a successful career in the banking industry as a commercial lender, credit analyst and as the Director of Personnel and Training for a major regional bank holding company.

He holds a B.A. in Business Administration and is a graduate of the National School of Human Resources of the American Bankers' Association at the University of Colorado. Kevin is a Professional Member of the National Speakers Association and is listed in National Register's Who's Who in Executives and Professionals.

Kevin is the author of the best-selling audio programs, *"Coaching Skills for Managers and Supervisors,"* and *"Financial Fitness: How to Budget Your Time, Your Money, and Your Life."*

Contact Information:
Kevin Lust, CSP
Lust Development Group, Inc.
3208 Victoria Drive; Suite 202
Springfield, IL 62704
Phone: (217) 241-5877
Toll Free: (888) 241-5878
FAX: (217) 241-5879 • Cell: (217) 741-5878
E-mail: KevinLust@KevinLust.com
Web Site: www.KevinLust.com

CHAPTER 9

Motivating the "Bad Attitudes"

BY MICHELE MATT, CSP

Michele Matt is an awesome writer and speaker. She exudes the most important traits of a motivational leader; enthusiasm, intelligence, and relentless determination. Michele, very simply put, will make things happen through the power of sheer determination and perseverance. I would want her on my team every time.   – VO

*   *   *   *   *

A single idea, if it is right, saves us the labor of an infinity of experiences.
– Jacques Martitian

Motivating the "Bad Attitudes"

By Michele Matt, CSP

I f you think it's tough motivating yourself to change behavior or achieve a goal, try influencing someone who has a bad attitude! One of the greatest challenges facing today's leaders is motivating the people who resist change, defy authority, and avoid taking responsibility.

People with "attitudes" are everywhere … at work, home, school, and on the highways of our life's journey. Some attitudes are great to be around while others are extremely challenging.

As the author of the best-selling book *Attitude: The Choice is Yours,* I have worked with the good, the bad, and the downright ugly attitudes. I have noticed that attitudes affect virtually everything we think, feel, say and do.

To motivate someone who has a bad attitude, first understand these two principles about people: attitude is a choice, and for every action, there is reason and reaction.

PEOPLE PRINCIPLE #1
Attitude is a Choice

Life is full of choices. You choose where you live, where you work, and what you do in your free time. Likewise, you choose what you think about and how you feel about yourself, people around you, and things that happen to you. To gain control of your life, you need to make positive choices about your attitude, relationships, and situations.

PEOPLE PRINCIPLE #2
For Every Action, There is a Reason and Reaction

You do what you do because of your past experiences, current knowledge, and beliefs about the future. Your parents, teachers, mentors, and society have influenced how you behave around others. Therefore, you — and other people, too — do or say things for a reason. Even so, it is very natural to have a reaction — positive or negative — to other people's behaviors.

Knowing these two principles helps you understand what motivates people to action and why you respond the way you do to other people's behavior. Unfortunately, you can't make others do what they don't believe is important. You can, however, choose how you respond to or influence others and their attitudes.

Your Natural Response

How do you feel when you are around someone with a bad attitude? If you're like most people, your responses may include *frustrated, angry,* or *depressed.* You may respond by avoiding that individual — a natural reaction when someone complains, yells, or simply does nothing. Let's face it. It feels emotionally draining to be around someone at work, at home, or in public who has an unpleasant attitude.

For instance, a manager feels frustrated with an employee who whines about having to complete a specific task. A worker feels irritated with a co-worker who doesn't pitch in to get a job done. A parent gets angry with a son or daughter who argues or sasses back.

Your Options

In some extreme cases, dealing with someone who has a bad attitude can stir feelings of being trapped or helpless. However, when it comes to handling these situations, you do have some options. By using the following five steps for dealing with a bad attitude, you will learn how to:

- Feel more tolerant of other people's behavior
- Understand what's important to the person
- Positively impact their behavior
- Resolve conflict or confusion
- Regain your positive feelings

Step One: Determine Your Involvement

When you encounter a bad attitude, your first step is to determine if you will say or do anything about the situation. This step involves a preliminary assessment of your feelings including the importance of the relationship and the impact the attitude or behavior has on the situation. To accomplish this step, ask yourself these four questions:

1. Is the relationship important to you?

The answer would most likely be "yes" if the relationship involves a family member, friend, co-worker, boss, or customer.

117

The answer would most likely be "no" if it involves a stranger you met on the street, at a party, in a store, or on the highway.

2. Has the person said or done this before?

The answer would be "yes" if you observed this person's negative behavior at least once before.

The answer would be "no" if this is the first time you have heard or seen this type of behavior from this person.

3. Does the behavior bother you or others?

The answer would be "yes" if you or other people have strong feelings (i.e., anger, frustration, etc.) about the attitude or behavior.

The answer would be "no" if you choose not to let the other person influence how you feel about him/her or the situation.

4. Should you invest your time?

The answer would be "yes" if you believe it is within your responsibility to better understand the other person and perhaps even influence his or her actions.

The answer would be "no" if you believe it is not appropriate for you to discuss the situation with the person. This could stem from a number of reasons, such as:

- You could be in a public setting and may not want to embarrass the person in front of others. It is always better to confront someone in private, if possible.

- You may have had previous conversations about the person's behavior, yet he/she continues to behave inappropriately. In this case, you may need to take more extreme measures or forget about it; consequences will eventually catch up to the individual.

If you answered "no" to any of the four questions, you have the option to remove yourself from the situation. You can *physically* remove yourself by walking away without saying or doing anything, thereby avoiding the situation. Or you can *mentally* remove yourself by choosing to not allow this person's actions to bother you. Either way, removing yourself from the situation may be temporary or permanent. For instance, you may choose to take a temporary "time out" to collect your composure or information about the situation — or you may decide you have more important things to worry about.

On the other hand, if you answered "yes" to each of the four questions, you have confirmed the following: the relationship is important to you; he/she has said or done this before; the behavior does bother you or someone else; and you believe it is appropriate to become involved in the situation. In this case, move to the next step.

Step Two: Understand the Situation

The purpose of this step is to better understand why a person acted in a particular way. Because we often initially think the worst before learning the facts, this step will prevent you from making incorrect assumptions about the situation.

To accomplish this step, ask the individual open-ended questions to explore the rationale behind his/her attitude or behavior. The most effective fact-finding questions begin with who, what, when, where, why and how? For example, ask:

> *Who* was with you?
> *What* happened?
> *When* did you do it?
> *Where* were you?
> *Why* did you do it that way?
> *How* did this happen?

By asking these types of questions, you will learn the reason for the behavior. You might be surprised what you learn! For instance, an employee named Chris came to work two hours late. At first, his supervisor Pat thought Chris has a tardiness problem. However, after asking a few open-ended questions, Pat learned Chris just had a car accident. How often do you think the worst about someone until you learn more about the situation?

For a variety of reasons, people don't do what *you'd* like them to do. In his book *Why Employees Don't Do What They're Supposed to Do*, Ferdinand F. Fournies describes the results of a 15-year study of employee nonperformance. According to the study, employees don't do what they're supposed to because:

1. They didn't know *why* they should do it.

2. They didn't know *how* to do it.

3. They didn't know *what* they were supposed to do.

4. They think your way won't work or that their way is better.

5. They think something else is more important.

6. There are no consequences for poor performance.

7. There is no recognition or appreciation for good performance.

8. There are obstacles beyond their control.

9. They have personal limits that prevent them from performing.

10. No one could do it.

Except for the last reason, there are specific strategies you, as a manager, parent or teacher can use to help people perform successfully and meet your expectations. Provide open, honest, complete, and ongoing communication. Use this type of two-way communication to explain, train, recognize, and coach people to influence their behavior at work, at home, or in the classroom.

After learning the reason(s) behind the person's behavior, ask yourself one more critical question: "Do I still want to make a change?"

In some cases, you may learn the other person didn't know what was expected and/or you may need to give him/her the proper training or tools to do the job. However, if you are still concerned about that person's attitude or behavior, move to the next step.

Step Three: Influence His/Her Attitude or Behavior.

This is probably the most challenging step in this process. It is extremely difficult for you to change your *own* behavior, let alone the behavior of someone else. But managers, parents, and teachers can use any of the following three strategies to motivate a difficult employee, co-worker, spouse, or teenager toward positive behavior:

1. *Describe how you or other people feel.*

   You have the right to feel angry, sad, or frustrated about another person's attitude. Sometimes letting that person know how the behavior made you feel can influence a change. Perhaps the person simply wasn't aware of the impact the behavior had on others.

2. *Explain potential consequences.*

   If you tolerate poor performance, you'll get poor results. Clearly communicate potential consequences to the individual. For instance, let an employee know what may happen if his/her performance doesn't improve (i.e., verbal warning, written documentation in the personnel file, or termination). As a word of caution, don't share meaningless threats if you aren't prepared to follow through. One of the quickest ways to lose credibility is to not do as you promised.

3. *Suggest other ways to think about the behavior.*

Let the person understand how his/her behavior affected a project, another department, a person, or the reputation of the organization. Describe how his/her attitude may have caused other people to react negatively. Help the individual realize how important his/her positive contribution is to the situation's end result.

Unless the other person takes responsibility for his/her actions, the problem remains yours. Once you gain his/her agreement that it is important to make a change in attitude or behavior, move on to the next step.

Step Four: Solve the Problem

Problems or frustrations occur when something doesn't meet your expectations. For instance, you expect an employee on the job or a teenager at home or school to do "good work." But how well do you describe your expectations to that employee or student?

Be specific. To describe when something needs to be done, many people use sloppy terms like "whenever" or "as soon as possible." Unless you provide clear expectations, you set yourself up for disappointment. Therefore, the next time you ask someone to do something for you, describe it in specific terms:

What does/doesn't need to be done?

Who needs to do it?

When does it need to be done?

How, if there is a preference, should it be done?

Working together with the person, develop solutions and steps to resolve the problem. Determine what action will help to improve the situation.

Step Five: Recover

After your discussion, regain your positive attitude about yourself *and* the other person. Most important of all, acknowledge that conflict is not bad or wrong. It is *how* you deal with conflict that matters most. Managing conflict in a positive manner can help both you and the other person understand what is important to each of you, as well as help you both agree on the best way to resolve the conflict. Remember, you *can* enjoy a positive relationship with a negative person; it may be helpful to separate the person from his/her bad attitude.

Generally speaking, men deal with conflict in more positive ways than women do. Two men can be at odds with how something should be done, talking openly and even loudly about the situation. In the end, they agree on a resolution and go on with the "business" at hand without hard feelings. On the other hand, when women are in conflict, the situation is not pretty. If a woman has a problem with another person, she may either:

> Hold a grudge
>
> Avoid communication
>
> Complain to other people

None of those strategies resolve the conflict. Conversely, each one further complicates the situation, challenges the relationship, and stifles communication. Ladies, if you have a problem with someone else, do yourself a favor and either confront the person to resolve the problem or forget about it. Some women carry grudges for so long, they can't even remember what caused the original problem! That type of unresolved conflict can fester within and may even lead to health problems.

Nurture Growth

The key to making any long-lasting changes in another person's behavior is to encourage and praise positive performance. Unfortunately, we often use the "no news is good news" philosophy for communicating with others. This lack of communication leaves our employees, co-workers, children, and even spouses feeling neglected or unappreciated.

People are like plants. A healthy plant is well cared for with proper lighting, water, and fertilizer. If the plant is kept in a bad environment or not properly cared for, it may wilt and die. Likewise, people are motivated when they are nurtured and stimulated in a positive environment.

If you want to bring out the "best" in even the "worst" of people, sprinkle them with words of praise and appreciation. They will react more favorably to you than if you constantly criticize them.

In Summary

Being around negative people at work, home, or school can put a real strain on your level of motivation. In fact, bad attitudes can deteriorate the morale of the most upbeat, positive people. As a manager, parent, teacher, friend, or spouse, it is your responsibility to learn how to motivate individuals who have bad attitudes to communicate and interact with others in a more positive manner to achieve positive results.

Each person is unique and has different priorities and preferences. Therefore, what motivates one person may not motivate another. However, if you can learn how to use this five-step process for dealing with difficult attitudes, you will appreciate and accept the:

Choice of attitudes and actions you take in life

Relationships you share with other people

Results you get from things you and others say or do

Use these ideas to channel the power within yourself and others!

* * * * *

Michele Matt, CSP
Phoenix, Arizona

 Since 1984, this best-selling author, nationally-recognized speaker, and training consultant has inspired the attitudes and actions of people all over the world. Each year, she conducts dynamic keynote presentations and workshops at conferences, for organizations, schools, churches, and even prisons. Regardless of the type of audience she is working with, Michele has the ability to challenge minds and touch hearts. She is an expert in helping clients get **R.E.A.L.** results with their people – **RETENTION** of employees and customers, **ENTHUSIASM** to take **ACTION** and **LEADERSHIP** to make a positive impact!

In 1991, she founded *Inspiring Solutions* in Des Moines, Iowa and in 2003 she moved the business out to Phoenix, AZ. She has provided motivational leadership in several professional associations including the American Society for Training and Development (ASTD) and National Speakers Association (NSA). Michele is one of 5500 international distributors for Inscape Publishing – the creators of the DiSC profile and other learning instruments to help hire, manage and serve people.

Michele is a Certified Speaking Professional, an award given to less than 10% of speakers worldwide. She has published 4 books, 3 training videos and several resources on the topic of attitudes, leadership, customer service, and strategic planning. Her first best-selling book, *Attitude: The Choice is Yours* is now in its sixth printing.

Contact Information:
Inspiring Solutions, Inc.
17338 W. Imperial Lane • Surprise! AZ 85387-7540
Phone: 866-225-1249 • Fax: 623-322-3852
E-mail: Michele@InspiringSolutions.com
www.MicheleMatt.com
www.InspiringSolutions.com

CHAPTER 10

Looking at Time Through the Lens of Leadership

BY LAURA STACK, MBA, CSP

Laura Stack is the most organized and talented person around. This comment is made by everyone who meets her. If you ever are in doubt as to what is one of the most powerful skills for success, look no further than Laura Stack. Her success is a powerful affirmation for the value of organizational skills ... coupled, of course, with immense talent. The value she delivers to everyone she works with is immeasurable.   – VO

* * * * *

Drive thy business or it will drive thee.
– Benjamin Franklin

Looking at Time Through the Lens of Leadership

By Laura Stack, MBA, CSP

G ood leaders in the year 2000 and beyond understand that time management is not about squeezing more into their days. As a leader in your organization, you must do one thing very well with regard to time management — you must help your folks spend their time productively toward the accomplishment of organizational goals.

This chapter will help you realize this objective by discussing three key time management principles for leaders: (1) keep employees from burning out, (2) model effective time management behavior, and (3) eliminate activities that waste time. With these principles, you can lead yourself and others to use time more wisely.

Principle #1. Don't Overload Your Folks

When you have key employees who work hard, long, and effectively, you naturally delegate important projects and tasks to them — lots of them. That's understandable, because you trust them. "Give it to Judy, and it will get done." Unfortunately, your over-zealousness and confidence in your superstars can burn them out if left unchecked. As the workload increases beyond the point of manageability, satisfaction, quality of work, and effectiveness decrease.

Many employees will take on an increased workload *temporarily* to meet a key project deadline or launch an IPO for a new dotcom with stock options. However, if that level of work goes unabated for too long, an employee's effectiveness will diminish. If employees don't take care of themselves, they will have no energy to devote to work. Dan Miller, 38, is the CEO of BuyingDecisions.com — and a father of six kids. "I could just dedicate myself completely to work," he says. "But if I do that, my marriage suffers, my kids suffer, and I suffer. I've learned that when you don't have balance in your life, then you end up getting stressed out. You bring that burden and conflict to work with you, and then you can't be as productive."

A colleague shared with me his experience consulting with a startup organization. The leader was a fairly new manager, there were critical deadlines looming, and the organization was having a hard time staffing vital positions. The leader kept delegating project after project to the existing employees, forcing many of them to work until 1:00 a.m. each day to meet the deadlines. They burned out, left the company, and the entire launch went belly-up without these key personnel. If building instant fortunes means treating people like machines — bringing in next year's models when they burn out — the best and the brightest will eventually look elsewhere.

Watch for the warning signs of burnout in your employees:
- Excessively long working hours for extended periods of time
- Fatigue
- Clock watching

- Distractedness
- Acting like a broken record
- Problems in their personal lives
- Withdrawing from social relationships
- Depression
- Substance abuse, or
- A strong desire to head off to the South Seas with a paintbrush in hand

Don't be responsible for putting somebody over the edge! Listening to your folks will provide a great return on your investment of time and energy. Find out what's working, where they are overloaded, and when they have too much on their plates. Don't allow them to wear "no sleep" like a badge of honor.

Action Items:

- Make sure that you're sharing the load with your other employees. In many large consulting firms, for example, analysts and consultants get assignments from a number of different partners. It's often hard to determine how much work people have on their plates at any one time. Employees just accept most projects, because billable hours tend to equate to value in the firm. The result is often unlimited work and burnout. To combat this, one consulting firm — Ernst & Young — established committees to review time sheets to ensure that no one person was overburdened. "There are a lot of type-A personalities who will work themselves to frustration and then quit," said Jeffrey Calvello, 33, a senior audit manager. In 1999 alone, the committees reduced the workloads of 48 people, sometimes without their knowledge. E&Y knew that ultimately this was simply good for business.

- One of the best retention strategies today is to recognize an employee's need for flexible scheduling, working arrangements, and work sites. You must help employees juggle the family balance issues they struggle with daily. By doing so, you gain their focus while on the job and dedication to the company. In addition, many of the younger "Generation X" workers today highly value their personal time and private family life, so workload becomes a retention factor. It's not enough to offer your employees free coffee and stock options. There has to be a human side to working at a company or people won't stay. You could allow telecommuting, implement compressed work weeks, add satellite offices for people with long commutes, offer paid time off for volunteer or charitable work, or provide leaves of absence for employees who need a break.

- Work with your clients on creative ways to get the job done in a less harried fashion. If someone must be on-site at all times, you can stagger the work schedules, so that one person works Monday through Thursday, taking Friday off, and another works Tuesday through Friday, taking Monday off. Convince clients to change their mindsets. Turnover in your firm is their problem too.

Principle #2. Model Effective Time Management Behavior

Model the things you expect from your people, so that you are a source of inspiration rather than a cause of resentment. How can you create a culture that respects work and family balance, for example, if you don't demonstrate it yourself by your actions? How motivating can it be to have an employee request a piece of information, to have you take 30 minutes finding the paper in the piles all over your desk? How can you say professional growth is important, if you don't spend any time talking with your employees to help them determine how to be successful?

Employees frequently complain that the boss doesn't plan well and has them running in a million different directions — chasing the latest crisis that the boss actually created. "A lack of planning on your part does not constitute an emergency on my part," read the sign on an employee's wall in my client's office. As the leader, it's tempting to put things off until the last minute because your staff can drop everything and bail you out. When you refer to yourself as being "under the gun," are the problems of your own making? Did the gun appear after your failure to attend to business in good time? Instead of being proactive early, you procrastinated until the due date became a crisis deadline. Then your folks paid the price.

Also model appropriate balance in your work and family lives — don't try to be Super Person. There will always be more things to do than there is time to do it. Focus on your highest priorities and figure out how to eliminate, delegate, or simplify the less important.

Action Items:

- To reduce time spent by your staff on crisis management, spend time doing long-term, proactive, important activities, rather than always responding to the urgent. Don't facilitate crisis at work by procrastinating on tasks until they become urgent. Leadership in time management requires you to: (1) figure out what matters most, (2) empower yourself and others to develop the abilities needed to accomplish those important objectives, (3) remove obstacles to their accomplishment, and (4) eliminate procrastination. Ask yourself: what ideas, projects, and programs — if implemented now or in the near future — would significantly impact the profitability or productivity of your staff or your organization?

- Invest the time and energy in setting up an organized system to sort, filter, process, and organize incoming information from multiple inputs. Hire someone if you need coaching on organizing your workspace, email, conversations, and paperwork. Why? First, perception — studies show that people often equate sloppy work areas with incompetence and indecisiveness. Second, opportunity cost — it's been estimated that the average professional spends 36 minutes a day looking for things. That's time much better spent on important tasks or getting out of the office earlier.

• Model a healthy balance to employees. If you're holding a meeting or conference out of town, invite the spouses as well. If your son is having a little league game or your daughter is testing in karate, take comp time, and openly leave the office at 4:00 p.m. to show your commitment to your family. Once in a while, leave your office at lunchtime if you have an important personal issue to handle. Or hit the company gym a few days a week. Read a book, think quietly for a time, or talk with a friend about an idea not related to business at hand. Get a life! Let your employees see that you are a real person, just like they are.

• Take care of yourself — physically, emotionally, and spiritually. If you don't, your ability to take care of others will decrease as well. Figure out where you are out of alignment with your values. Does your time reflect the things in life that are truly important to you? Keep asking yourself questions: "What's bothering me?" "What's happening to me that I don't like?" "What am I tolerating?" Figure out what you don't need to do in your life and quit doing it (watching television, PTA, hire out the housework, etc).

Principle #3. Control Timewasters

Another primary leadership responsibility with regard to time is to determine how you can remove things that waste the time of your people, as well as things that interfere with the achievement of organizational and departmental objectives.

IBM, for example, wanted its employees to move faster, make decisions faster, and complete projects faster, to compete with the hungry startups that were gnawing on the edges of its business. Employees were so used to operating in the status quo, they were unsure exactly what that looked like. So IBM established a "Speed Team," consisting of successful project managers who had a strong reputation for pushing projects forward at a blazing pace. This team educated IBMers on the characteristics of fast-moving projects and taught them how to eliminate "Speed Bumps" — things that wasted time. These included administration, unnecessary levels of bureaucracy, too much red tape, and unclear priorities.

What are *your* speed bumps and how can you eliminate them? For Xerox, it was the reams of paperwork required in the promotion process. For Procter & Gamble, it was product testing to the nth degree before introducing and marketing new products, which it discovered didn't work on Internet time. For Jason Olim, CEO and President of CDNOW, it was his former entrepreneurial mantra: if you don't do it, it won't get done right. For Timberland, it was the reluctance to admit that the processes that you've worked so hard to perfect may no longer be valid.

Ensure YOU are not the speed bump — the causal factor in wasting your employees' precious time. How are you the thorn in their sides? A common area is forcing employees to attend too many meetings, with too little relevance, that waste too much of their time. Reportedly, Robert Crandall, former CEO of American Airlines held all-day meetings with very few breaks. Was that really necessary? Were these meetings worthwhile?

In addition, consider *when* you hold meetings. Corporate America has trained most people to be "morning people." Our natural energy cycles cause us to be "up" or have "prime" time first thing in the morning. Unfortunately, most managers insist on holding meetings at that time. Prime time should instead be spent on difficult activities, important decisions, and complex

135

tasks. It's costly to have your key people tied up in routine meetings during periods of peak energy and productivity.

If unclear priorities plague your team, you must take action to resolve the confusion. Employees often complain, "I cannot get anything done during the day, because my manager is constantly interrupting me, having me chase the next fire, or reshuffling my priorities." Or conversely, YOU are unable to get anything done because your employees are constantly interrupting you with trivial matters.

For example, I talked with a manager at Coca-Cola who truly wanted to maintain an "open door" policy with his staff, but he was plagued by constant interruptions when working on key deadlines. He was torn about carving out time to complete urgent tasks, while at the same time creating an environment that welcomed and was receptive to employee questions and concerns. So he devised a plan to use a signal with his staff ... a red baseball cap. At the next staff meeting, he explained his dilemma and plan. When he would prefer to not be interrupted, he would put on a red baseball cap. If an employee noticed the cap, the person should determine if their issue was truly an emergency or if it could wait until later. He also encouraged his staff to interrupt him one time for five issues, rather than five times for one issue. The manager reported that the number of interruptions decreased by simply pointing out the difficulty he was having, and the red cap worked beautifully.

Action Items:

- Only schedule morning meetings if they involve brainstorming or complex problem solving. Hold staff meetings or project updates in the afternoon. Or, try not to meet at all. Come up with alternative ways to share or distribute information. If the meeting does not require problem solving, brainstorming or input from employees, and is simply informational in nature, why do you have to meet face-to-face? Could you send out a group voice mail, an email, or a memo? Or ask your staff to submit their updates and project status in writing one week prior to a conference call. Then simply include the relevant information from the responsible employee right in the agenda. Ask if there aren't any questions, then move to the next item. Keep meetings focused, tangent-free, and moving.

- Create a "Communication Log" for each subordinate, on which you record tasks and information updates as you think of them. Have a five-minute "stand up" meeting with each person once (or twice, if necessary) a day to delegate new work, prioritize, update, and refocus. Get up and meet in your employee's office, because you can leave more easily. It's often difficult to remove someone from your office chair once the person is comfortable and in talking mode.

- Agree on a "signal" with your folks to cut down on interruptions. You can use orange arm bands, police tape, a name plate turned face down, a "be back at" clock on the door, a miniature desktop flag...it doesn't matter what the signal is, as long as everyone understands and abides by the rules of engagement. Obviously, you can't wear your red cap 100% of the time, or people will begin to ignore your signal.

Conclusion

To make the best use of this chapter, identify the single most important thing that you could do — immediately — to make a difference in the way you handle time. Plan a way to implement this change or help others to reach this goal. Ultimately, the best leaders can create in others the competency and ability to manage time wisely, in accordance with established goals. Always be asking your folks, "How can I help you be more productive?"

Henry B. Eyring says, "Time passes at a fixed rate, and we can't store it. You can just decide what to do with it — or not to do with it... Your inheritance is time. It is capital far more precious than any lands or houses you will ever get. Spend it foolishly, and you will bankrupt yourself and cheapen the inheritance of those who follow you. Invest it wisely, and you will bless generations to come."

*　*　*　*　*

Laura M. Stack, MBA, CSP
Highlands Ranch, Colorado

 Laura put the "PRO" in "PROductivity." She helps people leave the office earlier, with greater energy, and more to show for it. She is the President of Celebration Presentations, a time management consulting firm that caters to high-stress industries. Her customized keynotes and workshops focus on tightening personal productivity, managing multiple priorities, balancing work and family, getting organized, and reducing stress. Laura is known for her high-energy, high-content, interactive approach in presentations that entertain, educate, and motivate people to improve. Laura's client list reads like a Who's Who of recognizable names, including Qwest Communications, Time Warner, Lockheed Martin, Lucent Technologies, Coca-Cola, Wells Fargo, and McDonald's, plus a multitude of associations and governmental agencies.

Laura is the youngest businesswoman in the history of the National Speakers Association (NSA) to earn the Certified Speaking Professional (CSP), a designation awarded to less than 7% of its international members. Her unique background as a corporate organizational development consultant, University of Colorado instructor, CareerTrack speaker, radio talk show host, actress and singer, newspaper columnist, and small business owner allows her to present dynamic, content-rich presentations that touch the heart and soul with practical, real-life information.

Contact Information:
Celebration Presentations
9948 S. Cottoncreek Drive • Highlands Ranch, CO 80130
Phone: (303) 471-7401 • Toll Free: (888) 284-7325
Fax: 303-471-7402
Email: Laura@LauraStack.com
Website: www.LauraStack.com

CHAPTER 11

Leadership Strategies in Customer Service

BY BERNADETTE TRUJILLO-VADURRO

When you meet **Bernadette Trujillo-Vadurro**, you know there is something special about her. She has that "fire" in her eyes. The biggest reason that she is such a gift for her audiences and her friends, is that she is able to impart that "fire" to everyone she meets. True motivational leaders always have that fire burning within them. Bernadette is one of the people who helps light those fires.   – VO

* * * * *

All the darkness in the world cannot obscure the light of a single candle.
– Dr. Martin Luther King

Leadership Strategies in Customer Service

By Bernadette Trujillo-Vadurro

"I'd rather fight than switch!" This was the mantra of an old cigarette commercial declaring customer loyalty.

Competent leaders and managers are challenged to discover how to instill this type of customer loyalty. Understanding how to meet this challenge is not only necessary, it is essential to the success of every business leader. This chapter focuses on how to create a customer service-focused environment that motivates customers to this level of loyalty.

Six essential elements are needed to create this environment:

1. Show commitment to your employees.

2. Trust and empower employees to do the right thing.

3. Allow and learn from mistakes in your organization.

4. Obtain feedback from your internal and external customers.

5. Hire, train, and retrain.

6. Provide recognition, rewards, and celebrations.

1. Show Commitment to Your Employees

Several studies demonstrate a direct correlation between how an organization treats its employees and how its employees in turn treat the organization's customers. Top performing companies, such as General Electric, Disney, Southwest Airlines, and Intel understand this correlation well. In these companies, managers, team leaders, and supervisors go the extra mile in creating an organizational culture that nurtures its workforce. Employees who feel respected, valued, and cared about by management are apt to demonstrate higher levels of customer service competencies.

For example, Intel employees are given significant benefits: paid sabbaticals after seven years of service, paid educational leave, generous compensation packages, etc. During a visit to Intel, I found employees to be passionate and dedicated in their work, as well as open to improved work methods. Their commitment to customer service excellence in product development and service was witnessed at every level within the organization.

Several organizations show commitment to their employees through simple acts like stocking the refrigerator with free drinks, allowing extremely flexible work schedules, designating every day as a casual business dress day, allowing employees to bring pets to work, offering take home meals and/or by providing onsite child care. Others show commitment through more complex acts like allowing work teams to organize themselves and determine their own project priorities, deadlines and budget. According to a *Fortune* magazine article entitled "Welcome to the New Company Town"[1] one company reported for every $1.00 spent on employee services, it yielded $1.75 in increased employee productivity. Leaders and organizations that show commitment to their employees enjoy such benefits as exceeded deadlines, larger profit margins and lower staff turnover.

Several years ago I worked with a small but extraordinary company on leadership development. This company had just been bought out and employee morale was quickly deteriorating. The employees of this company had previously enjoyed many internal perks including frequent training programs. One by one these initiatives began to disappear. When the new management decided to stop providing free beverages and began charging employees for the onsite child care program, the employees felt totally betrayed and within two years, the organization lost a substantial number of its brightest employees. At the end of a 2-year period, product innovation had decreased substantially, and profits had flattened.

2. Trust and Empower Employees to Do the Right Thing

Southwest Airlines, hailed as one of the most innovative and profitable airlines in its industry even in recent difficult times, is a leader in understanding the core ingredients of creating a customer service-focused environment. Authors Kevin and Jackie Freiberg report in their book *Nuts*[2] that the culture of Southwest Airlines is designed to meet the employees' needs first.

---

1 Useem, Jerry. "Welcome the New Company Town." *Fortune*, January, 2000.

2 Freiberg, Kevin and Jackie. *Nuts*. Austin: Bard Press, 1996.

As a customer service industry giant, Southwest Airlines shares with its employees the "do the right thing" philosophy, meaning staff members are encouraged to make decisions using their best judgment. Such a philosophy sends a powerful message to each employee: "Management TRUSTS you, management BELIEVES in you, and management EXPECTS you to do whatever is in the best interest of not only the customer, but also yourself and the organization." Wow! By promoting this philosophy, Southwest Airlines successfully prevents a common industry obstacle, which is the fear of failure. Many organizations still tightly hold onto the reins of decision-making, fearing that empowering employees to "do the right thing" may result in overnight bankruptcy or incorrect decisions. In actuality, such an attitude hampers productivity and morale.

I once heard a colleague remark, "Employees buy homes, raise children, make investments, participate in community service, and make many important decisions. Yet when these employees walk through the doors of the company, it's like a great big suction machine renders them brain-dead and they forget how to make decisions."

I believe this suction machine is akin to a phenomenon found in many organizational cultures where employees are powerless because of an underlying current of paranoia. In organizations where employees feel powerless, customer service becomes a frustrating experience. Customers tend to get passed from one employee to another in an attempt to resolve a problem or obtain information. Employees in de-powered organizations use phrases such as "I don't know," "we can't," or "it's not my job."

An example of a case of customer service powerlessness, with catastrophic results, occurred when a fire in New Mexico destroyed more than 47,000 acres of forest, some of the Los

Alamos National Laboratory and 240 homes in the town of Los Alamos. It was reported that an employee of the National Park Service contacted the Forest Service to request assistance with a prescribed burn that had gotten out of control at 3:00 a.m. The Park Service employee was informed he would have to call back at 8:00 a.m. when a supervisor would be available to authorize assistance. By the time the Forest Service sent firefighters out at 11:00 a.m., the fire was horribly out of control. Had these employees been trained to transcend the rules to "do the right thing," assistance would have been sent immediately and a disaster likely avoided. Many organizations give lip service to empowerment; true empowerment means that employees are free to make important decisions on the spot with the information provided.

3. Allow and Learn from Mistakes in Your Organization

During my seminars, I frequently ask participants what normally happens when someone makes a mistake at work and how the mistake is dealt with. Their answers are always strikingly similar. They speak about a tendency to deny responsibility for mistakes, to place blame on someone or something for the error, or — most often — to cover up or hide the mistake.

Management guru Tom Peters says if you are not making any mistakes, you probably aren't doing anything at all. So, will some bad decisions be made? The answer is yes, occasionally. But an occasional bad decision can help educate the rest of the staff. Healthy organizations allow and learn from mistakes. Leaders in these organizations hedge their bets by providing employee education and training, yet are aware that mistakes *can* and *will* occur. A true customer service-focused environment means working in a culture in which mistakes are part of the learning process.

In her program called How to Lead a Team[3], Sheila Paxton, describes an interesting example of coaching and mentoring. Using the illustration of a gymnastics coach spotting an athlete, Sheila draws the analogy that coaching requires a solid presence to provide physical support, mental guidance, and a safety mechanism for the gymnast should she fail to make a jump. In this sense, many industry leaders fail because the initial coaching and mentoring needed to develop employees is not furnished. Leaders often are penny-wise and pound-foolish when it comes to proper staff training. In effect, subordinates are asked to walk the balance beam, try a few flips, and do some back bends with only a handshake and a hearty "good luck." Mentoring and coaching employees are time consuming initially; however, the end result is competent and proficient employees who are, in the long run, much more productive in their jobs.

4. Obtain Feedback from Both Internal and External Customers

Internal customers are our own valued employees. It amazes me just how much information our own employees gather and store. Organizations can save thousands of dollars that might otherwise be spent on consultants, surveys or focus groups by asking front-line employees three simple questions: 1) what is the number one issue, problem, or concern our customers complain about, 2) how can we improve service, and 3) what policies, processes, or procedures stand in the way of excellent customer service?

Smart companies encourage employees to provide management with feedback. But what separates a good organization from a great organization is its management's ability not only to gather information, but, more importantly, to make changes

---

3   Paxton, Sheila, *How to Lead a Team*. Boulder: Career Track, 1996.

based on the feedback received from its internal customers. In fact, those leaders who truly listen to their employees frequently get a jump-start on their competition. Because employees have their finger on the customer service pulse, they can use this information to make quick changes in service or product specifications. What stifles employee feedback is either the "shoot the messenger mentality" whereby leaders shun the employee for giving negative feedback or the "ignore mentality" whereby the feedback is dismissed. When employees are confronted by either of these reactions to feedback they quickly become discouraged and stop providing it.

Responding to feedback from external customers is also vital to creating a customer service-focused environment. To find out how we can exceed customer service expectations, we need to talk with our customers. I highly encourage managers to embrace feedback gained from external customers, whether it comes from complaints, surveys, user groups, or focus groups.

We have all had frustrating experiences while dining out. I would like to share one of my experiences at a popular national seafood restaurant. Upon our arrival we were informed there would be a short wait before we could be seated. After about ten minutes we were shown to our table. Seated, we proceeded to wait another twenty minutes before anyone came to bring water, take our drink order or even bring table settings. I asked two separate waitpersons for assistance before going to see the manager. The manager assured me our service would improve. Needless to say it did not. While the food was excellent, the service was pathetic. Even though three different waitpersons waited upon tables in our section, only our assigned server was allowed to assist us.

After dinner, I again asked to see the manager as we waited for someone to pick up our bill. I suggested to the manager that the restaurant needed a new system for serving customers in a more timely fashion. The manager quickly denied this was the problem. He promised, however, if we returned and talked with him personally, he would ensure us a prompt waitperson. We decided not to return, as we had dined at this establishment several times and each time we had been disappointed with the service. This organization failed to value customer feedback and to recognize a system flaw that encouraged dependence upon one employee rather than upon the entire organization.

5. Hire, Train, and Retrain

The Container Store, in 2000 was voted the number one company to work for in the United States by *Fortune* magazine[4], and it continues to place as a top company for employees to work at today. The Container Store hires employees whose attitudes and values harmonize with the company's philosophies and it places an extremely strong emphasis upon the recruitment process to ensure the right type of employees are hired.

Using innovative screening procedures, companies can make sure they hire the type of employees they want to represent them. For example, one strategy is to ask a job applicant to give a short presentation to several other job applicants. All candidates are placed in a room and observed by managers. What the applicants believe they are being rated on is their presentation skills. In reality, the management team is rating the other candidates in the room to see who is truly listening to the presenter. This screening mechanism is used by companies who want to make sure they hire employees who have excellent listening skills. Regardless of their presentation skills, the candidates who fail to listen to their colleagues are simply not hired. Understanding the importance of effective

---

4   Roth, Daniel. "My job at the Container Store." *Fortune*, January, 2000.

listening is a critical component in creating a customer-focused environment.

In all customer service-focused environments, emphasis is placed on training employees in the skills required to achieve the customer service competencies needed to thrive in our global market. Through training, employees can learn how to engage in positive customer service interactions, increase listening and communication effectiveness, solve problems, and discover how to deal with difficult customers.

6. Provide Recognition, Rewards, and Celebrations

Recognition, rewards, and celebrations are all extremely important in creating a customer service environment. One of my favorite sayings is this: "What gets recognized gets repeated." Many managers use the mantra "catch them doing it right," which means catch employees doing a job right and then praise them.

Using a variety of incentives to increase customer service performance is important. And giving employees praise and positive feedback is one of the most cost-effective methods to achieve that. The informal high-five and enthusiastic "well done" to the sticky note with handwritten praise from the manager to the formal letter of commendation from the CEO are all examples that can increase performance. Finding ways to reward employees can be creative and exciting. We tend to think of rewards as only monetary. However, imaginative managers use other incentives, such as passing out Hershey Gold Nuggets or a Pay Day Candy Bar for a job well done.

One of my clients celebrates customer service initiatives through hosting pizza parties and giving polo shirts emblazoned with the company's logo and the words "World Class Customer Service." The company gives away "World Class Customer

Service" earth-shaped stress balls and pens. Employees create a quarterly newsletter filled with customer service testimonials, initiatives, and contests. These combined activities are a daily reminder of their commitment and dedication to customer service.

Understanding what motivates your individual employees is essential. For one employee, receiving the opportunity to perform more complex tasks might be considered a reward while to another employee it might be construed as punishment. Customize your reward system based on what motivates your individual employees.

As you begin to create your customer service-focused environment, I encourage you to move away from the commonly held belief that most employees operate in a mediocre mode. Rather, believe that 100% of your staff operates in a mode of excellence. In the words of Goethe, "Trust people as if they were what they ought to be, and you help them to become what they are capable of being."

If your organization can rise to the challenge of creating a customer service focused environment, you will be well on your way to establishing customer loyalty, whereby your customers will declare, "I'd rather fight than switch!"

* * * * *

Bernadette Trujillo-Vadurro
Santa Fe, New Mexico

 Dynamic, energetic, enthusiastic and highly motivational are words audiences across the country use to describe Bernadette. Her vast experience in training and speaking are a tribute to her success story. Bernadette Trujillo-Vadurro is the President of Leading Edge Training Technologies and Speakerslive.com. She produces customized training programs using multi-media technology, accelerated learning techniques and industry specific content.

Bernadette has trained organizations such as the Chrysler Corporation, American Express, Los Alamos National Laboratory, Columbia Hospital Corporation, Indian Health Services, Pittsburgh Housing Authority, the CIA and many more.

Her topics include World Class Customer Service, Thinking Outside The Box, Change Management, Professional Presentation Skill Building, Motivation and Attitude Improvement, Stress Management, Communication Skills and Leadership Training.

Contact Information:
Bernadette B. Trujillo-Vadurro
Leading Edge Training Technologies and SpeakersLive.com
821 Paseo de Don Carlos • Santa Fe, NM 87501
Phone: (505) 983-8986
Toll Free: (800) 736-8986
FAX: (505) 986-0055
E-mails: B@Speakerslive.com • Berna@letraining.com
Web Sites: 1) www.Speakerslive.com
2) www.letraining.com
3) www.BernadetteTV.com

CHAPTER 12

Leadership: The Tao of Humor at Work

BY TIM GARD, CSP

The ability to laugh and find humor in any situation can only be the result of an indomitable spirit. **Tim Gard** has an indomitable spirit. The ability to <u>make</u> others laugh and to teach others to find humor in any situation imparts the gift of that indomitable spirit unto others. Tim Gard is able to give this gift of laughter, and yet he gives so much more … he gives a piece of his own spirit to all he touches.   – VO

* * * * *

Once you get people laughing,
they're listening and you can tell them
almost everything.
– Herbert Gardner

Leadership:
The Tao of
Humor at Work

By Tim Gard, CSP

There was a time when everyone believed our earth was flat and the sun revolved around the earth. It took leaders like Christopher Columbus to take a stand and prove "everyone" wrong by taking risks and sticking to his convictions.

Along the same lines, there was also a time in the working world when everyone believed if you were laughing or having fun, you weren't working. Humor had no place at work. It took leaders like Norman Cousins, C. W. Metcalf, and Patch Adams to prove "everyone" wrong again.

During the last 10 years, only cave dwellers would have missed learning how humor helps people physically and psychologically. Humor is also shown to improve morale, self-esteem, and productivity in the workplace. Very few dinosaur thinkers still believe the earth is flat … or dispute the positive influences of humor in today's workplace.

The question is no longer if we should use humor as a relationship skill — but rather, how can we best use humor in a leadership role. In fact, today's true business leaders openly recognize humor as another skill that can be learned and developed, just as they develop negotiation or organizational skills. They know if they are to *remain* leaders, they must use the right tools to get the job done, serve the customer, market the business, and perform customer service. They won't just *survive*; they want to *thrive* in today's fast paced global economy.

However, it's interesting that as I share my "Developing a Comic Vision©" seminars, I am consistently asked, "As a leader, how do I use humor at work and still be professional?" It's a good question.

The Tao of Humor

For me, the "Tao" or the way of humor is quite clear. My connection with it goes back to 1974 when I was serving onboard the USS Midway CVA 41 in Japan. During that time, I learned that Japanese people call the way or path to something the Tao (pronounced dao). They believe the Tao leads to enlightenment. Many years later, I discovered this Tao definition fits my Comic Visions® philosophy exactly. I have been on the path of humor all my life. That's why I named my business Comic Visions, a term and philosophy that fits my own way of life.

In a nutshell, having a comic vision is choosing to use humor as a skill and choosing to act and not react to the situational stress encountered every day. It all boils down to choices. Some choices lead to anger and stress, but choosing the Comic Visions "Tao" leads to good humor and laughter.

Perhaps it would be best to view choice in a Good Humor Flow Chart like this:

158

The Tao of Good Humor Flow Chart

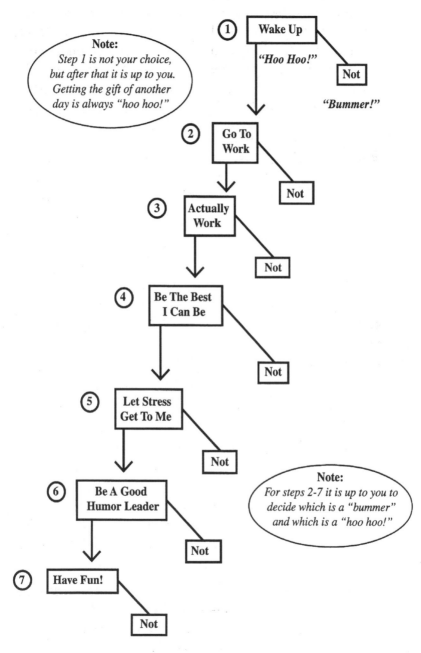

Note:
Step 1 is not your choice, but after that it is up to you. Getting the gift of another day is always "hoo hoo!"

① **Wake Up**

"Hoo Hoo!"

Not

"Bummer!"

② **Go To Work**

Not

③ **Actually Work**

Not

④ **Be The Best I Can Be**

Not

⑤ **Let Stress Get To Me**

Not

Note:
For steps 2-7 it is up to you to decide which is a "bummer" and which is a "hoo hoo!"

⑥ **Be A Good Humor Leader**

Not

⑦ **Have Fun!**

Not

You see, I believe our days are a series of choices just like in the flow chart. In our lives, we encounter good things and bad things; our problems often stem from only focusing on the bad things and not celebrating the good things. The bad things I vent by saying "bummer" and the good things I celebrate by saying "hoo! hoo!"

So many times we fail to celebrate the "hoo hoos." Instead, we take the bummers and stack them up one on top of another until we become one of those people who repeatedly say in a threatening way "TALK TO ME LIKE THAT, I'LL TALK TO YOU LIKE THAT!" I'm sure you've encountered them from time to time.

Just as standards are required for humor in schools, churches, synagogues, or any civilized gathering, humor at work has some guidelines, too. Unfortunately, they are rarely written anywhere. That is where following the Tao comes in.

Free Speech Quiz

First, answer this question: Do you have the right of free speech at work in the United States today? Some of you are shaking your heads and saying No. But the true answer is Yes. We have the right of free speech, but we also have the *responsibility* of free speech at work. That is, my constitutional right to say something at work does not supersede someone else's constitutional civil rights at work.

What's the difference between free speech at work and at home? It's simply this. At home, if a family member, friend, or neighbor tells a joke or says something inappropriate, we can simply walk away. At work, if we suddenly leave a meeting or go home because someone tells offensive jokes, this is called "quitting" or Absent Without Leave (AWOL). The right of free speech cannot take priority over co-workers' or employees' civil rights.

As we all know, we could be sued civilly or criminally for violating someone's civil rights, both in and out of the workplace. It's a fact: *we live in a litigious society*. Twenty years ago, who would have ever believed a person could go to the drive up at McDonald's, purchase a cup of hot coffee, drink that hot coffee, spill it and burn herself, then sue McDonald's because the coffee was "too hot" *and* win a seven-figure settlement? Who would have ever believed a criminal could break into your house, attempt to rob you, then fall over a piece of your furniture, break a leg, later sue you and win? It is beyond belief, but both scenarios are documented events. Someone could sue over almost anything. We must be aware of that — not afraid, but aware.

Unintentional Use of Humor

People bring humor to work in many forms: jokes, cartoons, internet humor ... the list is never ending. All this humor comes with only one filter applied: that it's funny. When something is funny, people want to share laughter with others. That's it.

But although humor may have a positive impact on the workplace, problems arise when people either intentionally or unintentionally misuse humor at work. Misuse happens in the form of unauthorized copies on office equipment, lewd internet messages, racial jokes, and much more. It is critical to recognize that bad humor at work can cause pain or stress. Good humor, on the other hand, may *come from* pain or stress but it does not *cause* pain or stress at work.

Certainly humor, used strategically, can be a powerful and positive force for good at work. However, used inappropriately or negatively, humor can be a source of stress and even EEO complaints. Simply asking, "Can't you take a joke?" after using bad humor does not make it acceptable. Especially be aware of the "accidental" or unintended audience around you. Although I have seen many really funny cartoons targeted toward human services professionals, I would advise against posting potentially offensive cartoons that poke fun at internal and external customers in office cubes or waiting areas. My suggestion is this: if you have to rationalize to yourself that something may not be appropriate at work, chances are it is not. As the saying goes, "when in doubt, leave it out."

Comic Vision Guidelines

The following guidelines help you use humor appropriately.

Comic Visions Tao Rule #1.
Understand that you don't have to tell jokes to use humor.

In fact, I believe jokes are the biggest source of trouble at work. Most jokes make fun of someone; we can easily offend without even knowing it. Use your own humor strengths. If you are an auditory person, then use more auditory humor. For example, I fly on airplanes quite a bit. Whenever I am boarding a late night flight or have had a particularly stressful trip, I stand in the jet way at the door to the plane and blow my wooden train whistle (sounds just like the real thing). Everyone laughs but, most importantly, *I laugh.* Then I board with a smile and feel much better. In this example, I had fun without telling a joke.

What if you are a visual person? Before my seminars, people commonly say, "I can't tell a joke to save my life so I can't use humor!" These folks incorrectly think they have to tell jokes to use humor. In fact, I believe we don't have to tell or even understand jokes to use humor at work, especially when they can be easily misused.

Instead, find some office visual toys that make people smile. Throughout my programs, I give examples of how to use ordinary items in extraordinary ways. For example, I have a hand puppet that looks like an orange crab. I call it "cube crab." I like to crab crawl along the top of a co-worker's cube with this crab. When the person sees it, I say in my best crab voice, "Are we being a little crabby today?" Then I run away!

Comic Visions Tao Rule #2.
Be a "good humor" leader.

To accomplish good humor, it's important to establish an "absence of malice" philosophy. In the workplace, I define absence of malice as being this: "A workplace where communication mistakes may happen, but no one ever intentionally uses humor to hurt or cause stress to another person at work." I am frequently asked what people can say (or cannot say) at work to keep out of trouble; I routinely answer that if you wonder if something is inappropriate, chances are it is. You can employ the CNN rule by asking, "Would you want to be quoted on CNN as saying what it is you are about to say?" Or make the "prudent person" philosophy prevail. "Would you say what ever you were going to say to your 9-year-old daughter or your grandmother?" Now ask how can you apply this philosophy at work every day, and do it!

Comic Visions Tao Rule #3.
Do any humor first for yourself, then share it with others.

Humor as a skill at work is like a humor "recess." When you were in school and went to recess, you didn't talk about schoolwork; you simply had fun. The same applies at work. Rediscover what makes you laugh and smile, then start there. When I was a state employee and later as a "fed" with USDA, I had to attend a lot of meetings. At first I was thrilled to be asked to participate. Then I discovered how boring they could be, yet I was not supposed to fall asleep. To survive the meetings, my co-workers and I used our Comic Visions in a variety of ways. For example, we played "Buzzword Bingo" (invented by Ben Yaskovitz and Laura Stern). We would take blank bingo cards and, in the squares, write all the words we knew would be said in the meeting in random areas. As they were said, we'd cross them off (just like in bingo) and declare a "bingo" by loudly clearing the throat.

I also encourage my audiences to do "mental magic" — those things we may *think* about doing but don't actually *do* at work. For example, in one really brutal meeting, I could see myself throwing my pen toward the door and saying "Is that my pen?" then walking up to the pen, picking it up, throwing it out the door and saying, "I have to get my pen" and leaving the meeting. I could hear my boss saying, "He'll be back, he just had to get his pen." Although I wouldn't do this, I have often thought it.

Comic Visions Tao Rule #4.
Be professional.

A professional will use just the right humor at just the right time. I encourage my audiences to be professionals who can laugh at themselves — as C.W. Metcaff says, "To laugh not with ridicule, but with objectivity and acceptance of self." That means, first and foremost, be a professional who strategically uses humor as a skill to improve your ability to do your job and enjoy life.

Work to develop this ability as a skill or business "tool" that professionals keep in their individual "toolboxes." For example, I'm not a stand-up comic or a clown; I'm a professional speaker who chooses to use humor as a skill in my seminars and my work. To do my job, I travel more than 100,000 miles a year and "occasionally" an airline will lose my luggage. I know this and am prepared. I carry a photograph of myself hugging my baggage. If my bag gets lost, I don't yell at the person in charge (what good does that do?). Instead, when they ask me what the missing bag looks like, I hand them the photo and lament, "We've only been together a few weeks." They always laugh and find my bag. I rarely get the photo back, though.

Comic Visions Tao Rule #5.
Timing is critical.

Your ability to use humor properly and strategically is the measure of your humor skill. When I was confronted with an angry client during my years as a fraud investigator, I couldn't always respond the way I wanted to when things that didn't quite "add up." Rather than carry that stress with me all day or say something inappropriate during the interview, I'd go to the break room later and read things like *776 of the Stupidest Things Ever Said* by Ross and Kathryn Petras. I'd laugh in an active attempt to vent my feelings, return to reality, and stop carrying the stressful situation around with me like baggage. This way, humor helps me renew myself between interviews and stressful encounters. I suggest you identify the situational stress factors in your job, realize they will not go away, then work to find Comic Vision solutions to them.

Comic Visions Tao Rule #6.
Establish your own Comic Vision tradition to close out your day.

At the end of every day, it's important to leave work and not drag the entire situational stress home with you. I suggest you end your work day by throwing your arms in the air and then performing your best impression of a gymnastic "dismount." And, as you leave your office, point at your desk and say "STAY." Most importantly, leave work at work; it awaits you the next day so you can "do that voodoo you do so well."

Having a Comic Vision harnesses the power of your unique sense of humor. More than anything, use it to have fun and be happier and healthier than ever.

Choose to use good humor and lead the way to laughter for everyone.

* * * * *

Tim Gard, CSP
Denver, Colorado

 Talented — Innovative — Memorable. Tim is fall-out-of-your-seat, tears-in-your-eyes, laugh-out-loud funny. But he's not a stand-up comedian. He is a gifted presenter who uses brilliant timing to skillfully weave memorable stories and playful moments into his outrageous presentations. Every fast-paced, interactive Comic Visions program gets people rolling in the aisles as they take away strategies to harness laughter. As a result, they learn to see the world through their own comic visions.

Tim's use of extraordinary props make him one of the most popular and original humorists on the platform today. His props are fun and funny but, more importantly, they serve as visual reminders to act — not react — to life's inconveniences.

From Singapore to Sioux City, Tim has been "cracking 'em up" as a professional speaker since 1984. As he says, "Remember, laughter becomes you."

Contact Information:
Tim Gard
Comic Visions®
4150 Ireland Street • Denver, CO 80249-8098
Phone: (303) 371-3311
Toll Free: (800) 865-9939
FAX: (303) 932-0990
E-mail: comicvisns@aol.com
Web Site: www.TimGard.com

CHAPTER 13

Why Leaders and Managers Fail

By Ruby Newell-Legner, CSP

Ruby Newell-Legner is the ultimate coach, whether it is in the sports world, the corporate world or in one-on-one situations. She is one of those people who truly helps others be better at what they do. She shares a combination of skills and talents to do this; enthusiasm, teaching, encouragement and altruism. The one guarantee when you encounter Ruby and her work: you will be better than you were before your encounter.   – VO

*   *   *   *   *

Always keep in mind that your own resolution to succeed is more important than any other one thing.
– Abraham Lincoln

Why Leaders and Managers Fail

Take an escalator ride to improving your supervisory skills

By Ruby Newell-Legner, CSP

Lisa had earned her recreation degree and all her certifications. Delighted to be working in her chosen field, she was hired to be in charge of the recreation center when her manager wasn't on premise.

A brand new, educated professional ... but it soon became clear Lisa wasn't doing her job well. Suppose you were her manager and had compiled a list of all the things Lisa had done wrong. You might have "dumped" this list at her 90-day review. But if you did that, everyone involved would have paid an undesired price. Instead, it's important to redirect her actions without dampening her enthusiasm — to act as a coach rather than a hard-nosed boss.

As the manager facing this dilemma, the "coach" approach worked well. Over breakfast, Lisa and I had an open conversation about her future success. By outlining the skills she needed to develop, spelling out examples of problems that occurred, and discussing how she could solve them proactively, we came to an understanding. That meant, for example, that two weeks before the Tae-Kwondo tournament, she should post a sign explaining that basketball would be canceled that day. Then people could avoid disappointment by not showing up for basketball on the day of the tournament.

Lisa began to see what skills she needed to be successful and started embracing the lessons we discussed. She has not only learned them; she adopted a winning attitude that led to several promotions. In fact, she is now a facilities manager on her own.

Most importantly, though, Lisa came away from her 90-day review knowing her manager wants to help her succeed. I came away feeling like a coach whose protégé had just won an important race. And so could you.

Too many so-called leaders and managers fail to energize their people and encourage them to build the careers of their dreams. If you ask those you manage what they want from you, their answers are simple (but not always easy to deliver). In the words of nationally known speaker Dr. Lloyd Lewan, chairman of Lewan & Associates (the largest provider of office technology in Colorado), they want you to "turn me on, keep me focused, and treat me right."

Managers and leaders who overlook these requirements fail because they:

- are poor role models
- never make it clear what they expect
- misuse their time on items of low priority
- don't talk to their staff in meaningful ways
- haven't helped their employees see the perceptions others have about them, thus affecting their credibility and ability to do their jobs well

If you struggle in your role as supervisor, manager or leader, ask yourself these five critical questions:

1. Are you a good role model?

2. Do your staff members have a crystal clear picture of your expectations?

3. Do you have efficient and productive time management skills?

4. Here's the biggie: Do you communicate all the information your staff members need in an appropriate way?

5. Do you promote professionalism by helping your employees develop the skills and confidence they need to feel successful?

Here are five responsive ways to deal with them. Follow these steps and you'll take an escalator ride to becoming a top manager.

1. Be A Good Role Model

At one point in my management career, I used to share an office with my boss. Consequently, each of us knew about every single thing the other person did.

One day, my boss came to me and said, "Ruby, you need to talk to your assistant. Yesterday, I saw him on the phone for more than 45 minutes on a personal call. He is not giving his job the priority time he should." Just as I stopped to consider how to deal with my assistant, I heard my boss pick up her phone and talk to her husband *for more than an hour*. With that action, she set a bad example as a role model and I lost a lot of respect for her. Walking your talk sets the standard for everyone around you, but *particularly* for those you manage.

2. Draw a Clear Picture of Expectations

Do you make time to tell those valuable people you manage what their goals should be? Do you ask for their input, their ideas, their feedback?

If you behave like a 90-mile-an-hour tornado all day long, when do your staff members talk with you? How will you ever create an open environment? When would you build relationships with someone new to your group?

Start simply. Decide what *one thing* you can do today to clarify expectations for each person you manage, and put each expectation in writing. Then look at the mission statement for your whole organization and for your group. Do your department's activities line up with each of the stated purposes?

To get clear on what's expected, outline specific tasks and behaviors, and inform them they will be evaluated on those tasks and behaviors. Tell them exactly *what* your organization's expectations look like and *why* they should adhere to them.

3. Improve Your Time Management Skills

Time management was extremely hard for me to learn as a "neophyte" supervisor. I would work 80-hour weeks and felt proud doing so. What dedication! Did I set myself up for wasting a lot of time.

Before you tire of overworking, use these time management tactics to help keep your sanity.

- Avoid having too many comfortable chairs in your office so visitors don't feel inclined to dally long.

- Make your phone calls more productive. Call your contacts at the beginning or end of the day when they are most likely to be around. Thursdays and Fridays aren't usually as busy as Mondays and Tuesdays.

- Make your phone calls in a "batch" to help avoid interruptions.

- Leave questions on phone mail so you get answers on the return call and help eliminate telephone tag.

- Decide what activities give you the most value. This visualization exercise changed my life: I see myself walking along a sidewalk and find some money on the sidewalk. Here's a one, five, ten. Over there is a 20 and over here is a 50. In a few steps, I see a 100-dollar bill. Which one would you pick up in this situation? I believe in picking up the 100 first because it's worth the most ... and walking by all the other opportunities. As you plan your day, pay attention to those "100-dollar-bill" activities and prioritize your day around completing them first. Then you can enjoy the highest return on your time investment.

You can use this concept when setting goals in your personal life, too. Every year on New Year's Day, my husband Rich and I review all our personal and business goals for the coming year. For example, on January 1, 1999, we set 66 goals and, by the end of the year, we had achieved all but nine of them. Each year, we post our list of goals on the refrigerator so we see them every day. Using the imagery of picking up 100-dollar bills helped us prioritize them. That's what being focused is all about.

I suggest you adopt a proven system that requires you to spend 10 minutes at the beginning of your work day to list and "view" all your activities, then assign A, B, or C priorities to them. From there, prioritize all the As, then the Bs, then the Cs.

With this time management system, you can stay focused even when an emergency arises. And you'll always know exactly where to get started again.

4. Communicate Appropriately — Biggest Need of All

When you communicate with the people you manage and lead, do you always take the same approach? If you do, then change your style … because people hear and respond to information in different ways. Using the style that best suits the person you're talking with gets the best results.

To understand many of these differences, let's take a trip to the zoo and meet five different animal types who, by the way, have human counterparts with characteristics that tell you their communication preferences.

Chameleons wear many hats, have good people skills and are open-minded. They can be flexible and may appear wishy-washy. Having a short focus, they like to do something fast and move on quickly. They roll with the punches, require flexibility, and thrive on change — a rare quality since only 7% of the population embraces change. On the down side, others find chameleons to be unpredictable and indecisive. They often don't know where they stand with chameleons.

Lambs are the non-conformists and peacemakers of the world. They're approachable and easygoing; they quietly get things done and aim to please everyone. If a project needs to be handled well, managers delegate it to people who are lambs because they are dependable and don't easily get distracted. They play the role of the "worker bees" in the organization. However, lambs have difficulty speaking up. Not very assertive, they can be called pushovers, wimps, and overly sensitive.

Foxes can be described with these words: skillful, playful, savvy, determined, observant, planners, sly, creative. Sometimes they are perceived as sneaky. They think outside the box and show good leadership qualities. People often go to a fox for counseling and insight. However, foxes can be jealous, stubborn, sly, overbearing, and too fast-paced. In addition, they're secretive and hard to "read."

Owls are the thinkers and mentors of the crowd. It may even appear they sleep during the day. Likely to act experienced and authoritarian, they are smart, reliable, observant, calm and intuitive. They listen well and often take a long time to make decisions. When people ask owls to decide something, they think through all the possibilities and make a sound decision. They teach patience. Yet many get frustrated with the owls' slow pace of analysis; they want to know NOW. And owls simply don't get things done quickly because they think too much.

Rhinos have a strong vision and can see where they want to go. When others get in their way, they face a Rhino's focused and driven energy. They have a mission in mind and expect people to get out of the way; their attitude appears to be "my way or the highway." Consequently, rhinos can be bullheaded and challenging to work with. (As a stubborn recovering Rhino, I am consciously adopting more of the lambs' traits to be more versatile and effective.)

Get to know the characteristics of the "animals" you manage and appeal to "what makes them tick" in your communications. Think about your personal style as a supervisor and be aware of the perceptions you leave every day.

Four Communication Phrases That Work

Taking a trip to the zoo leads to using a new language in your organization as you deal with people with different animal personalities than yours. Managers are wise to encourage those they supervise to use the following four phrases when dealing with people. Teach your staff to use these phrases to promote positive communication.

"Let me see if I understand you correctly." Then repeat what the other person has just said.

"What I'm hearing you say is _____." This helps ensure both people involved in the conversation know what has been communicated.

"Let me make sure I have this straight." This phrase is great to use in customer service situations.

"Does that sum up what you have told me?" This confirms you have all the correct information.

5. Promoting Professionalism in Your People

If the attrition rate in your profession or industry is high, that's scary and, I assume, unacceptable. What can you do to change it? Encourage people you manage to think about the "big picture" purpose of their jobs with these 15 reminders.

16 Reminders for Projecting a Professional Image

1. Keep these easy-to-use reminders in front of you every day.

2. What are the most important "100-dollar-bill" activities you will do today? **Set priorities daily.**

3. When someone confides in you, keep it between you and that person. **Confidentiality builds trust.**

4. Give employees opportunities to develop new skills that can replace bad habits. **Be developmental, not punitive.**

5. Moaners and complainers don't make powerful role models. **Show support for others in your organization**.

6. Things can still get done when others do not do it your way. **Be flexible.**

7. When those you supervise fail in performing a task, ask, "What did you learn?" and encourage a discussion or your employees will spend time beating themselves up. **Allow people to fail gracefully and learn from their mistakes.**

8. Sleep on big decisions. Reread your email before you send it. You leave a footprint as a professional on every document. **Be conscious about everything you do.**

9. If workers get berated by their bosses in front of customers, how motivated are they to return to work the next day? **Praise in public; counsel in private.**

10. You have to look like a successful leader before others treat you that way. **Dress professionally** to leave a professional impression.

11. "If you don't like your job, get out of that spot ... someone else wants it," says speaker and coach Sarah Reeves. **The more in love you are with your job, the more successful you'll be.**

12. You will enjoy the success of helping your employees grow. **Ask their opinions; don't tell them what to do** so they can learn as they go.

13. The more you **show your people you care for them** and connect with them as human beings, the more successful they will make you.

14. The faster you forgive yourself for making a mistake and learning from it, the less damage it will do. Take **ownership of your mistakes.** Be the first to tell your supervisors "I messed up — this is what I did, this what I learned, and this is how I will handle the situation in the future."

15. People in charge truly know who gets things done. **The less credit you try to grab, the more you are likely to get.**

16. People speak the loudest when they listen the most. The words "listen" and "silent" both use the same letters. When you listen and when you are silent, you get the same result. **Listen more than talk.**

Most of all, be a coach, not a judge, so the "Lisa's" in your life can build careers in a way that reflects your best supervisory skills.

Managers fail because they fail to make a difference in the lives they touch. Adopting a "coaching" attitude will accelerate your ride to the top. So help your employees grow. Let them shine. And when they do, their brilliance will reflect on you.

*   *   *   *   *

Ruby Newell-Legner, CSP
Littleton, Colorado

 Ruby Newell-Legner, CSP, offers teams, supervisors and front-line employees a "magical" formula for building valued relationships. Her high-energy keynote presentations and training sessions combine encouragement with skill-building strategies that participants can implement right away.

Ruby's expertise comes from more than 20 years as a teacher, coach, manager, and professional speaker. As a high school swim coach, she achieved 47 wins against only two losses. During her three years as a special education teacher, she helped seven students graduate — from a program that hadn't graduated one student in the previous 16 years!

In her career as an award-winning speaker and trainer, Ruby has helped participants on three continents refine skills that build rewarding relationships. She's recognized as a Certified Speaking Professional (CSP), a coveted designation awarded by the National Speakers Association, and was honored to be a featured speaker at the National Speakers Association of Australia in April 2000. Ruby's clients include MCIWorldCom, GE, Apple Computer, ADP, United States Armed Forces, and municipal governments.

Contact Information:
Ruby Newell-Legner, CSP
Everybody's Business
9148 Vandeventor Drive • Littleton, CO 80128
Phone: (303) 933-9291
FAX: (303) 904-2966
Web: www.RubySpeaks.com
Email: Ruby@RubySpeaks.com

CHAPTER 14

Vision & Missions: Waste of Time or Effective Tool?

By Tom Doane

Tom Doane is a consultant in the truest sense of the word. He is the type of person that you wish you could talk to every time you needed insight, advice or wisdom. It doesn't matter if it is business related or personal, Tom has that rare quality of being able to impart the perfect piece of information for the appropriate situation ... and he is able to do it in a highly entertaining and digestible way. What a combination.   – VO

* * * * *

You are not here merely to make a living.
You are here in order to enable the world
to live more amply, with greater vision,
with a finer spirit of hope and achievement.
You are here to enrich the world, and you
impoverish yourself if you forget the errand.
– Woodrow Wilson

Vision & Missions: Waste of Time or Effective Tool?

BY TOM DOANE

You have seen them. You walk into just about any local business, government office, or large multinational organization and there it is. In a frame on the wall hangs the mission statement — a.k.a. vision statement, core values, etc. Many times it is matted, framed, in color, and very impressive looking. Unfortunately, if you ask someone who works at the organization what the plaque on the wall means, most will develop a blank stare and answer with a simple "I don't know" or "some management thing, I guess."

For all that has been said about the importance of using a written Mission or Vision to build commitment among those in the organization, the reality is that far too often these efforts bear no positive results. Many times, in fact, they become a source of snickers and jokes.

Is the whole exercise of developing and articulating a shared direction simply a waste of time? Absolutely not!

Finger on the Pulse

As the first step in working with a 280 employee manufacturing company, I selected several people from various functional areas to interview. I wanted to put my finger on the pulse of the organization and develop an understanding of how employees viewed their jobs.

As I walked into the welding department on a hot and sticky summer afternoon, I saw a few men hunched over their welding jigs, sparks flying about, and decided to ask them about their jobs.

"What are you doing?" I asked the first man.

"I'm busting my back pumping out these parts; what's it look like?" was the reply.

I asked a second welder the same question. "Just working, man. Making $12.75 an hour to keep the family going," he said matter-of-factly.

As I approached a third welder doing similar work, I sensed a hard-to-describe "air" about him. He seemed to be going about his work ritual in a more purposeful manner than the others. I approached him and asked, "What are you doing?" The welder shut off his equipment, lifted his helmet, and with a fierce look of pride announced, "Me. I'm helping develop this place into a world-class outfit of craftsmen who make the best damn bicycles in the world!"

How would you describe the difference in the way these three welders spoke about their work? Which one would you like to work next to? Which one would you hire? The first two spoke in terms of action and of "self." The third spoke in terms of creating extraordinary results and of "others." Without having a professionally worded, beautifully framed mission statement, this person has committed himself to working toward a vision.

Managers want an organization full of people like the third welder. Developing and using a shared direction properly is the first vital step toward building this kind of commitment.

As you read the following benefits of developing and using a shared direction for your organization, ponder this question: "Why are so many outfits that have a mission or vision statement *not* experiencing these benefits (maybe even the organization where *you* work)?"

Benefit #1 — Provides a Compelling Reason to Offer Commitment

A shared direction describes the reason a group of people should want to throw their energy into coming together as a team rather than simply showing up for a paycheck. It provides a compelling reason for people to offer their commitment.

Every great organization — at least the truly successful ones — has a compelling reason for being beyond just making a profit. This is a core ingredient in developing true commitment in people's hearts and minds.

In their book *Built to Last: Successful Habits of Visionary Companies*, Collins and Porras describe the tangible results that companies with well-developed and well-used core visions (a.k.a. shared direction) enjoy over those without. The results run the gamut from higher market share and profits to recruiting and retaining more talented employees to developing breakthrough products and services, and more.

People in today's workforce look for a place to expend their efforts on something meaningful, something that gets their juices flowing. More and more, we find the best and brightest want to "develop this place into a world-class outfit" rather than "bust their backs making parts." They actively seek organizations that offer the potential to do so.

Benefit #2 — Paints a Picture of the Future

A shared direction paints a picture with words that provides a clear understanding of what the organization <u>will</u> be all about in the future.

To engage the hearts, minds, and hands of people at work, managers and leaders must help them articulate a believable view of how the organization *can* and *will* operate when it has evolved into its optimum state.

Washington D.C., August 28, 1963. On this day, in the shadow of the Lincoln Memorial, Dr. Martin Luther King gave one of the most electrifying and celebrated speeches of the century. His "I have a dream" speech was a powerful example of painting a picture with words of what a country could look like in the future. Mr. King was sharing a vision that day. The words he chose to use showed the importance of creating a vivid and exciting picture in the minds of those expected to work toward making the vision a reality.

Dr. King's voice did not boom from the podium: "I have a strategic plan!" or "I have some quarterly goals!" No, he touched the hearts of millions by sharing with them his dream. What's your dream for your organization?

It has been said that if you capture the hearts of people, their heads will follow. An effective shared direction should and can capture hearts by describing what a better future will bring. At the same time, the shared direction challenges their heads to find ways to make that vision real.

Benefit #3 — Provides a Common Reference Point

A shared direction provides a common reference point for all of the decision making taking place within an organization.

Currently, many organizations struggle with how to evolve from cultures of "command and control" in which management solves all the problems and makes all the important decisions to cultures of "engaged and empowered" in which employees share in decision making and problem solving. This transition can be confusing and stressful.

Roger, the president of a mid-size distribution company, shares a frustration typical of managers I have coached across many industries. He complains, "My people just do not seem willing to step up and make decisions, or at least offer ideas on how we can solve the problems we face. If they ever do, their input is way off base and focused only on what is best or easiest for them!"

At the same time, many of Rogers' employees tell me, "No way am I offering up any input or ideas again. Every time I make a decision without checking with management, I get creamed for it!" Sound familiar?

In working toward shared decision making and problem solving, it is vital for both management and employees to build trust and confidence in each other. A key element in building trust is knowing that everyone, from top to bottom, is using the same reference point when making decisions. A shared direction provides this reference point.

In organizations that have made the transition to "engaged and empowered," you will hear comments like these, which came from two employees of a small retail store in North Carolina:

"Regardless of my job title, I feel that I can and should act in the best interest of my customer and our company. I do not need someone's permission to make a good decision."

"At this place I do not need an OK from above to do the right thing."

Inherent in these comments is the fact that both management and staff have a clear and shared understanding of what "a good decision" and "the right thing" is. Specifically, the "right thing" is the decision that moves the organization closer to its desired destination — its shared direction!

Why Organizations Don't Experience These Benefits

Keeping in mind the potential value of having a shared direction, now ponder the question asked earlier: "Why is it that so many outfits that have a mission or vision statement do not experience these benefits?"

Blame two main culprits for this unfortunate but common situation. The first and most important relates to how the direction, mission, or vision for an organization originates. The following rather exaggerated account of a mission statement development process at a typical company provides some insight:

FollowTheCrowd Industries

The general manager of FollowTheCrowd Industries returned from the seminar with videos and books in hand. He immediately called a meeting of the executive committee and bellowed, "Every decent company around has a vision statement except us. We are going to change that! Next week, the six of us are going on a management retreat at the Surfside Resort & Spa to develop one of these darn things."

After arriving at the resort, the six executives worked for two solid hours hammering out the vision statement for FollowTheCrowd Industries before a brutal afternoon of golf and swimming. By Monday morning, the sparkling new FollowTheCrowd vision statement was framed and mounted on the wall in the main lobby.

The statement proudly proclaims that FollowTheCrowd Industries is the best company in the market, makes state-of-the-art products and services, supports the community, and views employees as its number one asset. Monday afternoon, the GM read the vision statement at an employee meeting and barked, "Make it happen, people!" On the way out of the meeting, employees traded smirks, rolled their eyes, and decided to wait for this latest fad to pass.

This outlandish example does bring to light a core problem with many organizations' mission or vision. If a few top executives are the only parties involved in its creation, is it a wonder no one else feels a sense of ownership in the direction?

The second culprit is that mission statements rarely become a part of the organizations' day-to-day work life. Rather, they simply remain the "plaque on the wall." If a vision or mission is not talked about, referred to, used in setting goals, brought up in coaching sessions with employees, and made an important part of daily decision making, it will never become the powerful tool it is meant to be.

For example, FollowTheCrowd Industries may boldly state in its vision statement "employees are our most important asset." At the same time, a new hire hears from veteran employees, "Yeah, we have an incentive plan here. If you screw up, you get fired!" Veteran employees know that when budgets get tight at FollowTheCrowd, the first thing to be eliminated is the investment in their development via training. Then at year's end, fat bonuses are paid to executives while employee salaries are frozen. The message becomes crystal clear that FollowTheCrowd only gives lip service to its vision.

When the organization's leaders do not act consistently with what is proclaimed, employees quickly become cynical towards the "plaque on the wall" and those who created it.

With all of this in mind, how can your organization reap the benefits and avoid the pitfalls of developing and using a shared direction?

Steps to Deliver Value

These basic steps have been helpful for several organizations that have created and put into use a valuable shared direction.

Step 1 — Develop the shared direction with everyone's input.

Explain to your employees what a shared direction is, why it is worth having, and how it will be used. Follow this with a series of small group meetings (4 to 8 people at a time) aimed at collecting their input regarding what the future should hold for the organization. Use this question to frame the discussion:

"If you woke up tomorrow and came into work to find that it had miraculously changed into the perfect place for both employees and customers, how would you describe it?"

In this perfect place:

What would employees say about the organization when talking with other employees?

What would employees say about the organization when talking about it with friends and family outside of work?

What would customers say about our organization?

What issues would we focus our energy on?

What would make us proud to be a part of this team and want to work here even if we were financially secure enough not to have to?

What am I willing to do to help us get there?

Capture all of the thoughts being shared in writing. Then create one or more teams (depending on the size of your organization) to sort through all of the input gathered at these meetings. Their objective is to search for common themes running through employees' input, write them down, and begin a process of sharing them back and forth with employees. Make sure this team represents a cross section of the organization with members from management and staff as well as different functional groups.

Creating the shared direction is only the beginning. It is critical to use the shared direction throughout the organization on a regular basis.

Step 2 — Set goals for each functional area or team.

These goals need to directly relate to closing the gap between where the organization is currently and where you have decided you want it to be. Especially take a hard look at the values you say are important that may not be consistently supported by actions and behaviors.

Examples:

- We say employee empowerment is important, but most managers behave like benevolent dictators.

- We say our customers are number one, but we make them jump through hoops if they have a problem with our product and need help.

Step 3 — Refer to the shared direction directly as often as possible.

When?

In staff meetings

During one-on-one coaching sessions

When making any decision ask, "What is the choice that moves us closer to the kind of organization we have described in our shared direction?"

Step 4 — Insist that managers talk about what the shared direction means to them personally with their team.

Then ask the team members what the shared direction means to them. To bring all of these ideas together discuss how the shared direction will be used to guide the team.

Step 5 — Schedule yearly "shared direction progress review" meetings.

The objective of these meetings is two-fold: first, it keeps the shared direction in everyone's mind, and, second, it offers an opportunity to celebrate progress and uncover opportunities for new goals.

Today's leader has many roles to play: coach, administrator, and motivator to name just a few. Choosing which priorities to spend your valuable time on can be confusing. So if you want to be the leader of a team of "world-class craftsmen" rather than a group of people "pumping out parts," make the development and effective use of a shared direction a top priority.

What is your vision?

* * * * *

Tom Doane
Raleigh, North Carolina

 Tom Doane is the founder and president of Performance Innovations Consulting Group, Inc., a firm with a strong reputation for delivering sustainable improvement in customer service, leadership development, team building, and creative problem solving. Tom operates his firm, and encourages his client organizations to follow his lead, embodied by the credo:

"There is no traffic on the extra mile"

A Michigan State University graduate, Tom started the firm in 1992 after a successful 8 year career as a consultant with Steelcase, Inc., the number one office furniture manufacturer in the world.

Tom has created performance improvements for organizations in many markets including; retailing, distribution, manufacturing, professional services and government. Client organizations are both large and small ranging from a 29 employee retailer in Michigan to Microsoft, Andersen Window Corporation, and the City of Raleigh, North Carolina.

In addition to his main focus on intensive coaching of organizations, Tom brings a humorous approach to learning, off the charts energy, and interactive style to association meetings and conferences across the country.

Contact Information:
Tom Doane
Performance Innovations Consulting Group
12337 Amoretto Way • Raleigh, NC 27613
Toll Free: (800) 897-8113
E-mail: doanetom@aol.com

CHAPTER 15

From the Beach to the Boardroom – How Do You Motivate Someone?

By Vilis Ozols, MBA, CSP

I believe that every person possesses unlimited potential. The only key that unlocks this potential is maximum effort. The only way I cope with failure is knowing that I exerted maximum effort. The upside of this is that I have learned that if you follow this belief, you don't have to deal with failure very often.

– VO

*   *   *   *   *

*To be what we are and to become
what we are capable of becoming,
is the only end in life.*
– Robert Louis Stevenson

From the Beach to the Boardroom – How Do You Motivate Someone?

BY VILIS OZOLS, MBA, CSP

A manager surprises an employee from behind, taps them on the shoulder, and asks, "How come you're not working?"

The startled employee replies, "Because I didn't see you coming!"

In a leadership role, this comes dangerously close to illustrating how challenging it can be to motivate someone. The concept of motivating anybody can be profoundly arrogant and highly presumptuous. Just because you are a president, a manager, or a team leader, that doesn't mean you can motivate another person. Similarly, any parent or spouse who has tried to motivate a family member or friend knows how truly difficult it is to succeed.

We tend to think of motivating someone as a special gift that only highly paid professional sports coaches or dynamic "bouncing-off-the-walls" motivational speakers can bestow

197

upon willing audiences. The reality is somewhat different. Intuitively, we all know the only person who can motivate you … is you, yourself. The best that any one of us can do — whether as a manager or leader, parent or spouse, friend or teacher, or even as a motivational speaker — is to put tools and techniques in front of people. Choosing to use the tools or embrace the techniques becomes *their* decision.

Emotional and Logical Motivation

I believe that there are two components to motivation: One is the emotional approach and the other is a logical approach.

Getting motivated will always be a very personal choice. Not all ideas will work with every person; that is the nature of motivation. It's important to understand that different people will be motivated by different things. Consider the following concepts, both emotional and logical.

The Only Goal You Can't Accomplish

Back in your face … the harder the better … that's how we play.

I got paid to play a game. A game that many of us enjoy at a company picnic or during a visit to the beach. My version of the game of volleyball is a little different than your picnic version. In my game the ball travels over 90 miles an hour. Two grown men try to cover a court that was designed for 6 people. In fine beach sand that collapses under your weight … we jump up and down to smash a ball over an 8' net, while a bronzed, chiseled muscular specimen of a professional athlete uses every physical resource to slam that ball right back in your face … the harder the better. That's how we play.

I can measure my career in lacerations, scar tissue, broken noses, torn ligaments, and broken fingers … some mine

... some inflicted on others. My game is so intense that you see veins popping on foreheads, striated neck muscles, bodies stretched to absolute physical limits, and involuntary primal screams of pain or exertion on every play. I've played on beach sand baked so hot by the sun that you get blisters on the fleshy underside of your toes ... and yet you keep on playing. Sometimes they break and bleed, sometimes they don't ... either way you keep on playing.

I've played in matches where the next point is worth thousands of dollars. Maybe you've seen my version of the game, the huge three-story inflatable bottle of tequila or inflatable can of beer, the professional bikini contest between matches, the ESPN cameras and crew, hard bodies, soft bodies, big crowds and the leader board with recognizable names like Karch Kiraly, Randy Stoklos and Singin Smith. Sometimes my name was on it too, ... sometimes it wasn't.

My frame of reference, as a professional and Olympic caliber athlete, teaches that the foundation of motivation is emotion and that there really is only one goal that you can not accomplish.

I learned the secret when I was only thirteen years old at a volleyball clinic with the defensive specialist for the Canadian Olympic Team. He told me that I would have to get so good at playing defense that I had to realistically have a shot at getting to any ball, no matter where on the court it was, regardless of how fast it was hit, or how far away it was.

I must have betrayed some of my 13-year-old skepticism with a combination look of "there's no way that that can be the truth" and "if that is true there's no way in the world that anyone can be that good ... especially me."

Sensing my consternation, he then pulled me aside said words that over twenty years later I can still recall.

"Son, you have the potential to be an Olympic athlete." My heart soared. He was the first one to ever say that to me. "But the reality is that you really do have to be so good, that you can defensively get to any ball at all and keep it from hitting the floor. Judging by the look on your face you're concerned that you might not be able to do that. But there's also a secret. A secret to being that good. You have to believe, truly believe in every fiber of your heart, that the only ball you can't get to, is the one you don't go after."

There was incredible motivation coursing through me at that moment, knowing that I had the secret as I participated in the next defensive drill. I was flying through the air, bouncing on the floor and rolling on the ground, doing whatever it took to get to the ball. The other thing I remember most vividly was that once the motivational intensity had worn off, I experienced intense pain like never before; bruised elbows, knees and hips. You name it, it hurt. It's important to learn techniques to go with your motivation. There is an emotional and a logical side to motivation. It was a great set of lessons.

I measure my career success in a unique way. When I was playing defense and there was an opportunity to dive after a ball, sometimes my mind would tell me that there was no logical way to get the ball before it hit the ground. Throughout my career as an athlete my internal wiring as a result of that special clinic was simple; you go after every ball … even in situations where logic says, "This can't be done." Your brain must override the negative and say "try anyway!" That is my internal measure of success: You go for it even if you feel there might be no chance of getting it.

And every once in a while you actually get it. I will remember every single situation where that occurred as if it had happened yesterday. It is those plays that I measure my career by. This lesson applies to life as well. I can honestly say that I somehow never believed that I would, in my wildest dreams, author and publish a book. Intuitively, it just seemed too lofty a goal. The fact that you are reading this intrinsically verifies this very point. If you only do the things you <u>know</u> you are capable of you will be forever constrained by your fear and your doubts.

You've heard advice from the pool, the gridiron, the track and from the boardroom. Well, here's one from the beach; The only goal you can't accomplish ... is the one you don't go after!

Back in your face ... the harder the better ... that's how we play.

Is Money A Motivator?

Sometimes in leadership we need to take a more logical approach. The subject of employee motivation is often treated by motivational speakers, managers, and coaches as only a pure emotional effort. In my experience, leaders can get people on board more effectively when they supplement the "rah, rah," emotional side of motivation and implement systems and techniques to achieve the desired performance (and the great motivational speakers who do exactly that).

I came across some profound research in the area of employee motivation while in graduate business school. The research of Dr. Frederick Herzberg provides clues on how to set up systems that truly motivate others. In fact, in *Louis Rukeyser's Book of Lists*, Frederick Herzberg's book, *Work and the Nature of Man*, is listed as one of the "Most Influential Business Management Books of the Twentieth Century." Even with this distinction, many leaders and managers have not been exposed to his work.

Herzberg investigated the question: Is money a motivator? His answer, paraphrased, is this: Money is a huge motivator, but only up to a certain threshold. It varies from individual to individual depending on a number of factors and situations, including expected earnings, earning power, and socio-economic status. If you do not earn enough money to feed your children, you are probably below your threshold and money is a huge motivator. Therefore, you will be highly motivated to work two jobs to provide for your family. The majority of people in today's corporate world are earning beyond their "money as a motivator" thresholds and so money is not a motivator.

Herzberg's research then identified certain motivators as "hygiene factors." These hygiene factors include working conditions, nice office, safety and comfort, wages or salary. Those need to be in place as part of the job but they are not motivators; they are maintenance factors. However, if any of these factors are removed, an employee will lose motivation or leave the job. Many leaders mistakenly target only these tangible "hygiene" areas to try and motivate others. Consequently, they do not get the expected success.

So what are the real motivators, according to Herzberg? He says there are three keys:

1. Reward and recognition
2. Involvement in the inner circle
3. Sympathy to life/work balance

1. Reward and Recognition

The first motivator, reward and recognition, relates back to pioneer studies in psychology labeled the "Hawthorn effect" (1927-1933 productivity study in Western Electric's Hawthorne plant near Chicago. These early researchers discovered that their own presence affected the outcome of the study, or, put another way, as long as they observed and recognized employee efforts, productivity increased. The term "Hawthorne Effect" was thus coined to describe how leadership attention increases productivity). The Hawthorn effect research says if you watch and acknowledge the work that people do, they will work harder than if you don't.

Put this more simply and make this your leadership motto: *Attention increases productivity.* A common attitude I encounter in low-morale organizations is that employees feel the people they work for do not *know* what they do and do not *care* about what they do. If you want a powerful way to motivate employees, figure out how to assert those two issues. How can you let your employees know that you are paying attention to what they do and that you value what they do? Leadership styles can vary, but your job is to figure out how you can do this on an ongoing basis.

2. Inner Circle

Involvement in the "inner circle" occurs when you include a team member as an insider in your leadership decision-making and information-sharing. This is one reason new managers feel so driven and motivated after receiving a promotion; they have been initiated into the inner circle. As an example, the management practice of "Open Book Management" — when an organization's management shares financial statements with employees and allows their input to affect the numbers — puts this aspect of Herzberg's work into practice as a motivator.

When football coach Mike Shanahan overhauled the NFL's Denver Broncos, he involved future hall-of-fame quarterback John Elway, the offensive line players, and the pass receivers in the entire process of changing the speed, diversity, and alignment of their offensive play book. He worked hard to include them in the inner circle to solicit their complete buy-in as he revamped the system. Three years later, the Broncos were back-to-back Super Bowl champions. How can you bring your team or group into your leadership inner circle of decision-making and information-sharing?

3. Life/Work Balance

Herzberg's third motivator is termed as "sympathy" to an employee's life and work balance. This includes things like flex time arrangements, casual work attire, job sharing, or simply the flexibility to allow people to deal with the day-to-day personal or home issues in balance with their work. Employees often quit because their manager was intolerant of their personal or home/life issues. Any organization loses employees in one of two ways: they either quit and leave … or they quit and stay. Do you, through organizational policies and practices, allow for balance or harmony of home and work?

Innovative Approach

What happens when you incorporate these three themes while interacting with employees and striving to accomplish your organizational goals? Here is an example of an innovative approach a manager shared with me during a workshop I was conducting.

The leaders of an organization approached their manufacturing employees with a proposal, giving them full decision-making powers, and involving them in the process and the outcome. They said the record output the facility had ever achieved in a single day was 4,000 units. They said if the employees could produce the record output of 4,000 units by three o'clock in the afternoon instead of four o'clock, their normal quitting time, then they could leave their jobs an hour early and still receive pay for the full workday. In the process, they still had to meet all the appropriate quality standards.

The employees accepted the proposal. And what happened? The facility hit the record output for an amazing four out of five days, and continued to do so for an entire calendar year.

It worked because all three of Herzberg's motivators were present: reward and recognition, inner circle decision-making and communication involvement, and sympathy for balancing home life and work with the opportunity to leave early.

A Powerful Assessment Tool: Attitude and Motivation

Consider two criteria when you assess your group. First criterion: are your team members "good at what they do" or "bad at what they do?" As simplistic as this sounds, most people are naturally one or the other. The second key criterion is: are they "with me" or "against me?" This one is slightly more subjective. It is up to you as the leader to continuously communicate what it means to be "with you" by using concepts like mission, vision, values, direction, and philosophy to describe what it means to be "with you."

Four possible combinations stem from these two criteria:

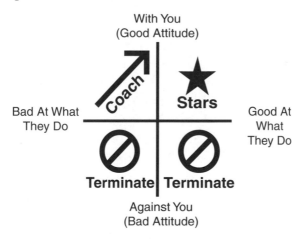

Each of these combinations has an appropriate leadership approach, summarized below.

Bad At What They Do + Against Me (Bad Attitude): These are the people who simply should not be with your organization. Terminate them. Alternately, you can set up a termination game plan including honest performance appraisals and corrective action schedules. With these people, a classic leadership phrase applies: It's not 'do you have the stomach to fire them?' It's 'do you have the stomach to live with the rest of your team if you *don't* fire them?'

Good At What They Do + With Me (Good Attitude): These are the stars of your organization — treat them like the stellar contributors that they are. Go out of your way to reward and recognize them, provide training, put them in a position to succeed, give them leadership opportunities, and offer them the perks and support that star performers deserve. These people will lead your organization into the future.

Bad At What They Do + With Me (Good Attitude): Coach, train, and invest in these people because they will deliver a very high "return on investment." Send them to training programs, set them up with a mentor, move them to more appropriate positions in the organization, and simply invest time and effort in them.

Good At What They Do + Against Me (Bad Attitude): This can be the most difficult leadership decision category. I suggest you terminate these people even more quickly than those in the first category. These folks will undermine and sabotage your efforts. You bend over backwards to please them, then end up worse off than when you started. If you can't terminate, "divest emotionally" from these people. Change your attitude and interactions with these types; do not allow them to take the emotional "pound of flesh" that makes your leadership job miserable.

Combine the emotion and the logic to put these systems, techniques, and strategies into action, and you are well on your way to being a motivational leader.

* * * * *

Vilis Ozols, MBA, CSP
Golden, Colorado

 Vilis Ozols is a former Pro Beach Volleyball tour competitor and a former member of the Canadian Jr. National Volleyball Team. In addition, he is a veteran business manager, an entrepreneur, and a gifted professional speaker. He is the President of the Ozols Business Group, a leadership training, motivational speaking, business consulting and publishing firm. He has held positions in sales, management, customer service, marketing and corporate training.

Vilis has earned the prestigious Certified Speaking Professional (CSP) designation awarded by the National Speakers Association held by only 393 professional speakers in the world. He is a past President of the National Speakers Association Colorado Chapter and was named their Member Of The Year in 2000.

Vilis holds a Masters Degree in Business Administration from the University of Colorado and he speaks to and trains literally thousands of business professionals every year. He has spoken in all 50 U.S. States, 9 Canadian Provinces, on 3 continents and in 8 countries. In addition to an array of Fortune 500 clients, he has taught creativity to Disney, leadership to the U.S. Olympic Committee and management skills to the I.R.S.

Contact Information:
Vilis Ozols, MBA, CSP
The Ozols Business Group
2002 Montane Drive East, Suite 3000 • Golden, CO 80401
Phone: (800) 353-1030 • (303) 526-2400
FAX: (303) 526-7562
E-mail: Vilis@Ozols.com
Web Site: www.ozols.com

Additional copies of
Motivational Leaders
can be obtained from any
of the authors.

*   *   *   *   *

Quantity discounts are available.

Did you enjoy the authors?
Additional products, services, links
and information can be found at

www.MotivationalLeaders.com.

- Do you have a company meeting?

- Does your organization have an annual event?

- Do you attend a convention that could benefit from one of these dynamic and powerful presenters?

Think about which author, story, strategy or philosophy spoke to you most clearly, and then feel free to contact that author, or any one of the authors, about having them present at your upcoming event.